TEACHING INTERCULTURALLY

TEACHING INTERCULTURALLY

A Framework for Integrating Disciplinary Knowledge and Intercultural Development

Amy Lee

With Robert Poch, Mary Katherine O'Brien, and Catherine Solheim

Foreword by Peter Felten

STERLING, VIRGINIA

Published by Stylus Publishing, LLC.
22883 Quicksilver Drive
Sterling, Virginia 20166-2102

Library of Congress Cataloging-in-Publication Data
Names: Lee, Amy, 1967- author.
Title: Teaching interculturally : a framework for integrating
disciplinary knowledge and intercultural development /
Amy Lee ; with Robert Poch, Mary Katherine O'Brien, and
Catherine Solheim.
Description: Sterling, Virginia : Stylus Publishing, 2017. |
Includes bibliographical references and index.
Identifiers: LCCN 2017009816 (print) |
LCCN 2017032585 (ebook) |
ISBN 9781620363812 (uPDF) |
ISBN 9781620363829 (ePub, mobi) |
ISBN 9781620363799 (cloth :alk. paper) |
ISBN 9781620363805 (pbk. : alk. paper) |
ISBN 9781620363812 (library networkable e-edition) |
ISBN 9781620363829 (consumer e-edition)
Subjects: LCSH: Multicultural education--United States. | College
teaching--Social aspects--United States. | Education, Higher--Social
aspects--United States. | Multicultural education--Case studies. |
College teaching--Social aspects--United States--Case studies. |
Education, Higher--Social aspects--United States--Case studies.
Classification: LCC LC1099.3 (ebook) |
LCC LC1099.3 .L434 2017 (print) |
DDC 370.117--dc23
LC record available at https://lccn.loc.gov/2017009816

13-digit ISBN: 978-1-62036-379-9 (cloth)
13-digit ISBN: 978-1-62036-380-5 (paperback)
13-digit ISBN: 978-1-62036-381-2 (library networkable e-edition)
13-digit ISBN: 978-1-62036-382-9 (consumer e-edition)

Printed in the United States of America

All first editions printed on acid-free paper
that meets the American National Standards Institute
Z39-48 Standard.

Bulk Purchases

Quantity discounts are available for use in workshops and for
staff development.
Call 1-800-232-0223

First Edition, 2017

CONTENTS

FOREWORD

In 1904, H. G. Wells published a short story called "The Country of the Blind." Wells tells the tale of an adventurer named Nunez who is unexpectedly dropped into an isolated community comprised entirely of people who are blind. Nunez marvels at how these people have constructed a world that allows them to live full and vibrant lives. Yet, as the only sighted person in the valley, Nunez assumes that naturally he soon will be king. Over time, he comes to understand that the country of the blind is not designed for those who can see, and the people of the community become increasingly worried by Nunez's peculiar behaviors and beliefs. Eventually, a doctor determines that Nunez's disordered mind results from his diseased eyes. To ensure Nunez can thrive as a member of the community, the doctor recommends surgically removing his eyes. Nunez flees.

This story invites us to notice that our fundamental assumptions about how our communities and organizations function are neither natural nor inherently good. Instead, as Ray McDermott and Herve Varenne (1995) argue, "every culture, as an historically evolved pattern of institutions, teaches people what to aspire to and hope for, and marks off those who are to be noticed, handled, mistreated, and remediated as falling short" (p. 336). As Nunez learns, sight is not an advantage in the country of the blind, and being blind is a disability only within cultures and institutions that are designed by and for people who can see.

Like the H. G. Wells story, *Teaching Interculturally* challenges us to be critically aware of our own "assumptions, ideas, and habits" (p. 10, this volume). These profoundly shape how we teach and who we are as teachers. We must attend to our own identities and beliefs as a necessary step in the often uncomfortable process of moving "from being simply a master of content to also being a non-master of intercultural pedagogy" (p. 41, this volume).

In an era when demands on faculty are many and resources are few, some may wonder whether that journey is worth the effort. Wouldn't it be simpler, perhaps even prudent, to stay within our disciplinary homes? After all, we are experts in our fields, trained to rigorously and creatively explore the world through the lenses of our disciplines. Isn't that enough?

In a word: No. To honor human diversity *and* to teach our fields (and our students!) effectively, we must develop and practice intercultural pedagogy.

As Amy Lee and her colleagues persuasively demonstrate: "you are teaching in and experiencing intercultural classrooms *regardless of whether* you want to, whether you are aware of it, and whether you think it is your responsibility or relevant to your discipline" (p. 15, this volume). Intercultural pedagogy is *not* an add-on to your course. It is a foundational component to all of your (and my) teaching.

Refocusing our teaching identities and practices through the lens of intercultural pedagogy may not be easy. In my case, I was trained to be a scholar of history, not a teacher. Fortunately, this book provides both a step-by-step guide and powerfully honest narratives of faculty who are making the slow but steady journey toward intercultural pedagogy. On this topic, Alison Cook-Sather (2015) wisely counsels: "In order to find empathy and understanding within oneself at the same time as one engages in the deep, critical analysis expected within higher education, [we] need to develop an awareness of [our own] assumptions [and] have patience—the ability to see that with time people [both students and faculty] may change or grow in unexpected ways" (p. 34). As this book shows us, employing empathy and patience as pedagogical tools is essential because what's possible in our teaching and our classrooms expands radically as we adapt our pedagogical orientation and practices.

Indeed, if we approach our teaching from a different cultural reference point, as the H. G. Wells story does, we may discover new possibilities for our students, our courses, and ourselves. In our classrooms, on our campuses, and in our world, we need more people who recognize that differing perspectives exist; that differing foundational assumptions are possible; and that there is value in critically evaluating ideas, problems, and structures from multiple angles. We need people who can recognize how and why our communities and cultures came to be the way that they are—and who can learn to function effectively within and, at times, to ethically act against those ideas and structures. *Teaching Interculturally* is a foundational text for that important work.

Peter Felten
Center for Engaged Learning
Elon University

ACKNOWLEDGMENTS

Amy Lee: This book is dedicated to John Magers and to my parents, Tom and Mary Gerry Lee—with gratitude and love. Thanks to Mike, Cathy, Jackson, and AJ for giving me a room with a view where both the first words and the final tweaks took place. Mary Katherine, Robert (Bob), and Catherine, thanks for making the project both possible and a pleasure. Thanks to Rhiannon Williams and Adam Jagiełło-Rusiłowski who lent their insights to the project in its early stages. Timothy, Elisabeth, Catherine, and Griffin: Thanks for feeding my curiosity, energy, and optimism. Finally, I am grateful to one of my first students, Andalib Khelghati. Andalib, your courage to question, your critical compassion, and your boundless commitment to justice and equity continue to inspire me.

Robert Poch: It is a great pleasure to acknowledge the advice, wisdom, and influence of the following undergraduate teaching assistants who improved the design and delivery of courses I taught over the last decade: Emily DePalma, Emily McCune, Julianna Ryburn, Jade Beauclair Sandstrom, and Chris Stewart. Also, multiple conversations with graduate research assistant Eskender Yousuf were instrumental in my teaching history and helped guide me to a manner that more fully honors and utilizes diverse student perspectives and lived experiences. Thanks are also long overdue for the life-changing intercultural mentoring I received in South Carolina from Julia Wells and Fred R. Sheheen. Finally, I remain grateful for the deep friendship, guidance, and encouragement of coauthors Amy Lee, Mary Katherine O'Brien, and Catherine Solheim.

Mary Katherine O'Brien: I want to first acknowledge Amy, Bob, and Catherine for being supportive, welcoming, and for inspiring me with their ongoing intercultural pedagogical development. For a new scholar, this group's commitment to authentic collaboration has set the bar very high for future partnerships. Completing this project would not have been possible without support from colleagues in the College of Veterinary Medicine and the Global Programs and Strategy Alliance at the University of Minnesota (U of M) or without the scholarly guidance I received in the UofM's Department of Organizational Leadership, Policy, and Development. I also want to acknowledge the impact of my practitioner colleagues in international education, who are often overlooked in this important work, and to honor the contributions of so many students who helped to shape my thinking over the years.

Catherine Solheim: I am grateful for the opportunity to participate in the U of M's Global Programs and Strategy Alliance's International Teaching and Learning Fellows program and the colleagues who initially invested in my development of an intercultural pedagogy and continue to support and affirm me in this ongoing process. I am deeply thankful for this team of colleagues—Amy, Bob, and Mary Katherine. I have found our two-year journey to write this book amazingly rich and productive. I am grateful for Thai family, friends, and colleagues who continue to teach me about crossing cultural boundaries. And last but not least, I thank the learners in my classrooms across the years who bring new perspectives and opportunities to learn and grow, who have pushed me to go deeper, and who have been quite forgiving when I've made mistakes.

PART ONE

INTERCULTURAL PEDAGOGY: FRAMEWORK AND PRAXIS

As we are writing this book, within a few weeks, the world has encountered countless mass tragedies, all of which were rooted in perceptions of and estimations about human "difference": the attack on the Pulse nightclub in Orlando, Florida; the killing of Alton Sterling in Baton Rouge, Louisiana; the killing of Philando Castile in St. Paul, Minnesota; the assassination of five Dallas, Texas, police officers; the mass killings in Nice, France. On our own campus, as on many others, students of color are worried about their safety when approached by campus and community law enforcement officials. Conversely, others in our community ask questions that link particular ethnicities and religious faiths to concerns about public safety. Further, current political rhetoric heightens tensions around human diversity as wall building between the United States and Mexico is debated and the loyalties of some citizens and new immigrants are doubted—once again—due to their faith affiliations and non-U.S. places of birth. With so many critical events happening domestically and internationally that expose the destructive potential of being ill-prepared to have difficult conversations about issues and problems with diverse stakeholders, we need intentionally developed pedagogical practices to engage diverse students respectfully and effectively within our classrooms.

Surely, higher education *as a whole* (not just those in cocurriculum roles, those in identity studies–related fields, or those teaching "diversity" courses) has a responsibility to help students *learn* how to approach, understand, and dialogue about complex issues and across diverse perspectives. Intercultural pedagogy offers a way to think about how your courses and teaching can support that endeavor in ways that are responsive to other demands on the course; intercultural pedagogy is not an "add-on" to an existing course but a way of thinking about how, what, and why you teach in ways that invite students to develop their capacity to effectively engage others and to undertake critical thinking. Classrooms are laboratories for learning *how to engage one another effectively while bringing the skills of critical thinking, revision, and discernment to bear.*

This book responds to the following particular intersecting realities of contemporary postsecondary education: (a) increasingly diverse students are enrolling in our institutions, and historically, institutions have not effectively supported the persistence-to-graduation for students from historically underrepresented groups; (b) historically, institutions and graduate programs have done very little to support faculty development related to teaching, or teaching that supports equity, diversity, or intercultural development; (c) faculty need theoretical and applied pedagogical models to support equity and inclusion in the classroom. The goal of the book is to support your capacity to develop an intercultural pedagogy, which includes practice, refinement, and reflection. In that spirit, we work throughout the book to help you develop a reflective stance on this work, to cultivate a repertoire of questions and strategies, and to practice an ongoing critical process in which to engage in this work with students. Part One, chapters 1, 2, and 3, focuses on developing a framework for intercultural pedagogy that is attuned and responsive to current contexts of postsecondary education. Part Two, chapters 4, 5, and 6, provides case studies and pragmatic tools to support the implementation of intercultural pedagogy in a way that is attuned and responsive to specific, localized—whether institutional, disciplinary, or programmatic—contexts.

1

FOR AN INTERCULTURAL PEDAGOGY

In fact, we do not even claim that we have managed to change or seriously challenge power relations in our own societies as a whole. What we have done, however, is introduce change in everyday local practices that we are involved in. (Katila, Merilainen, & Tienarirefer, 2010, p. 8)

We want to open this book simply. This book is *for* intercultural pedagogy. This book is *for* the argument that access is a starting point but is not meaningful without the requisite work to achieve equity and inclusion in higher educational contexts, which have functioned, beyond doubt, to foreclose both of those historically. This book is *for* taking seriously the intellectual and interpersonal challenges and dimensions of both intercultural and pedagogical work. We assume that you, too, are *for* these things.

We do not claim to advance a theory of intercultural pedagogy that will radically transform the deeply ingrained and troubling inequalities, injustices, enmities, and economic disparities that characterize contemporary global—and even U.S. racial—life and systems. However, we do seek to foster a deeper knowledge and skill base of pedagogical theory/practice and, in doing so, seek to advance a critical intercultural pedagogy that is capable of supporting a profound shift in daily local practice. We believe that a profound shift is necessary in the daily, local practices of teaching and learning in order to more fully utilize and honor human difference in higher education and to maximize learning in our classrooms.

We know that intercultural pedagogy cannot be contained, communicated, or covered within any single book, article, or workshop. It is a continual process of attunement, observation, reframing, failure, inspiration/motivation, and refinement. In this way, the concept of this book (supporting intercultural pedagogy theory/practice) is paradoxical. On the one hand, faculty need a guiding framework for intercultural pedagogy. We need shared and explicit commitments, values, and core principles to guide us and to use as a basis for organizing, assessing, and collectively engaging in this work. Without a guiding framework, one is left to ad hoc "good intentions," a piecemeal approach. One is also left without a community of theorist-practitioners with whom to dialogue and challenge ourselves.

On the other hand, any pedagogical framework needs to be nimble enough to support a range of disciplines and levels of teaching; flexible enough to be responsive to the experience, environment, and particulars of a given teaching and learning situation. Perhaps most importantly, an intercultural pedagogy framework needs to be restless and in process. It involves a dialogic relationship with practice, and practice is, by its nature, unpredictable, constituted by environments, participants, interactions, and contexts. Real teaching happens in complex and dynamic environments that involve real (and thus complex and dynamic) people who have different experiences and perspectives. A viable pedagogical framework will be one that provides a scaffold of key values that inform an intercultural approach. But it must be responsive to and not merely prescriptive or dogmatic concerning the interplay of theory/practice and concepts/contexts as described ahead (Lee, 2001).

Contemporary Contexts of Postsecondary Teaching and Learning

> Education in the twenty-first century must prepare students for a world that is increasingly interconnected, interdependent, and diverse. It is often difficult in such a world to communicate effectively, to form and maintain relationships and work cooperatively with people of different backgrounds. The need for these enhanced interpersonal skills across cultures is also evident domestically as U.S. society becomes more diverse. (Krutky, 2008, p. 3)

Throughout higher education in the United States, across diverse disciplines and types of institutions, we are experiencing rapid and even dizzying changes. As we identify a few of them ahead, consider how and which of them create tensions in relation to traditional structures and ways of operating. Notice how some create paradoxical (if not impossible) situations, and how many of these have emerged recently—within a generation of academic professional life.

- Pressure to standardize curriculum within and across institutions
- Emphasis on ratings, rankings, and assessments

- Emphasis on teaching less content and more "creativity, innovation, and problem-solving"
- Pressure to promote "volume" and efficiency in our teaching—whether via online courses or larger sections or in new forms of "intensive" degrees (weekends, evenings)
- More "market" competition in higher education; the use of the words "market competition" in higher education
- Decreases in governmental allocations, grants, and endowments for public and private institutions
- Unsustainable, exponentially increasing costs for attendance
- Pressure to cultivate new recruitment streams, including attracting more international students, largely from countries where the academic conventions of K–12 are quite different from those in the United States
- More students with language and cultural diversity from recent immigrant families

Many of us have multiple diversities present in any given classroom or academic program through increased domestic and global access to higher education. Others have more pressure to "teach diversity" or to achieve "diversity-related outcomes" given global economic interdependence. Many of our institutions have track records of failure or inadequacy in supporting or enfranchising students from historically underrepresented populations in our particular institution—students from low-income, first-generation, and/or racial/ethnic minority populations. In fact, in the last two decades, most of us witnessed an increase in access to our institutions for more diverse students but we have not achieved a correlating increase in success, whether measured by retention, graduation, or engagement data. Access is not the key to righting historical models of pedagogy and institutional organizations that do not equitably serve diverse student populations. Faculty intercultural development is a critical starting point, but it alone will not "transform" this institutional history.

Faculty recognize increased emphasis on learner-centered classrooms, student engagement, and active learning. There is more emphasis on student satisfaction; it impacts rankings, teacher ratings, and future alumni support. These are all increasingly important in a competitive "marketplace" of higher education. More of us are familiar with the idea that we *should* be "engaging" our students. But it is difficult to find evidence of systematic reform in terms of prioritizing and implementing formal initiatives that support faculty development to achieve those ends.

No wonder, given the dizzying pace of change and the absence of institutionally sustained faculty development opportunities, that we are not keeping up, so to speak. When we facilitated a roundtable on engaging intercultural pedagogy in undergraduate classrooms at the 2015 Comparative and International Education Society (CIES) conference, many of the attendees, though they spanned country-context, discipline, course level, distance and real-time classrooms, and institutional type, had the same questions. How can I establish an inclusive environment? How can I challenge my students to move out of habitual ways of thinking about difference so as to support their intercultural competence/cognitive complexity? How can I cover my required content while also supporting my students' intercultural/diversity development?

We noticed similar themes at the 2015 and 2016 NAFSA: Association of International Educators meetings in workshops, sessions, and roundtable discussions with administrators and faculty from diverse disciplines. At both venues, there was overwhelming frustration with disconnects between faculty intercultural competence and institutional expectation for faculty to function effectively in increasingly diverse environments. Indeed, the literature on intercultural education tends to focus on students' learning and development. Less attention is given to theoretical models, practices, and strategies to propel, deepen, and/or assess faculty's intercultural development or its synthesis/interactions with pedagogy. Hence, there is continued dissonance between setting expectations for student outcomes and ignoring or underemphasizing the need to enable faculty competencies to facilitate those outcomes.

> Amy often recalls the words of the new chair of her English department over a decade ago as he sketched his vision for a "robust, rigorous department." "Sophisticated work" by "people from good schools," more "critically sophisticated faculty" who "produce more" attracting "better" doctoral candidates who will be able to do "more interesting" work. I was puzzled by the complete absence of the words *teaching, learning, students, undergraduates, curriculum,* or *instruction.* (The emphasis on hazily defined "more" and "better" is likely familiar to most of us.) She asked, "Umm, where does teaching fit into this picture? Or students?" His response, "Teaching is a given."

Stenberg and Lee (2002) argued that this department chair's statement reflects a cognitive bias that needs to be unpacked and challenged. This book is dedicated to continuing that work of unpacking and challenging. Many factors, such as disciplinary/organizational norms, produce insularity, busyness, and oversimplifications that work against thoughtful and intentional engagement with learners. Intercultural pedagogy requires a process that is ongoing (not quick), intentional (not haphazard), developmental (not a singular event), complex (not simple), and integrative (not insular).

In contrast to this well-entrenched attitude that teaching is a "given" or a supplement to our "real" work, we refer to Lusted's (1986) conception of pedagogy as "the transformation of consciousness that takes place in the intersection of three agencies—the teacher, the learner, and the knowledge they together produce" (p. 3). Noteworthy in Lusted's conception is the integral relationship and impact among teacher, learner, and knowledge. He posits that the transformation of consciousness (which is critical to an intercultural pedagogy) does not occur without that collision.

In this book, our focus is on the teacher. Our intent is to support teachers in critically examining how they have learned to understand and to practice teaching, and to support reflection and revision that promote intercultural pedagogy. This book does not focus on the student or knowledge components of Lusted's triad, though both play a critical role. Rather, our goal is to dig deeply into the teacher element in ways that we hope will have value for teachers across different knowledge and institutional contexts and that invite you to actively deliberate about your particular disciplinary and student realities. We want to engage you in a process that leads to an intercultural pedagogy that is both viable and effective.

Supporting student learning and development begins with enhancing instructor knowledge and capacity (Lee & Williams, 2017). Although there is no one-size-fits-all or magical formula for this work, there are pedagogical principles and approaches, technological tools, and frameworks that scholar-practitioners find useful in supporting and utilizing the strengths of diverse student populations. Unlike investments in technology by which institutions demonstrate the capacity to create infrastructures, incentives, and training (Smith, 2010), there has not been a parallel investment in faculty development to support pedagogy, intercultural pedagogy, and diverse learners with longitudinal, resource-rich action plans. There are no indicators of institutional readiness in the arena of diversity. The need, incentives, rationales, and research needed to enact this readiness certainly exist. However, historical models for supporting faculty capacity to engage with diversity, equity, or intercultural awareness in the curriculum persist. We posit that they have been largely ineffective, often due to the "check-the-box," one-time workshop approach, rather than ongoing, systemic, institutionally sustained opportunities for faculty development.

Where we might first expect to see systemic change would be in the preparation of future faculty within doctoral programs. However, little evidence exists to suggest that doctoral programs support the development of doctoral students as teachers, let alone as interculturally aware teachers. Teaching development is not integrated in program requirements. We are not aware of doctoral-level qualifying exams that evaluate one's capacity to teach in addition to theory, content, and research capabilities. Even when teaching assistantships are available for funding and accruing experience, they rarely occur in the context of a programmatic approach to using that assistantship/practice to develop graduate students as educators, to generate reflection toward future and ongoing development. For many doctoral candidates today, just as for many of us in the last few decades, learning to teach . . . well, it just happens, if it happens at all.

This assumption creates many problems, chief among them the perception that one should or will be good at teaching if one "knows" one's discipline, and the concomitant cycle of blaming an individual (or students) if the faculty member isn't "good" at it. This assumption also renders us inattentive to teacher development in higher education, and to whether and how institutions are/aren't supporting teaching success. Positioning a highly complex capacity such as teaching (or intercultural effectiveness) as "natural" or "given" results in a system in which that capacity is not intentionally and systematically developed or prioritized in terms of resources and rewards. Thus, teachers are not likely to get the tools, time, and attention they need to develop and maximize their potential. This way of conceptualizing teaching's place and its value within the hierarchy of the "work" of professors envisions teacher development from a deficit model: if one shouldn't need to learn how to teach, those who actively seek to learn must have a deficit.

Why Intercultural Pedagogy?

As stated earlier, Lusted's (1986) definition of *pedagogy* is "the transformation of consciousness that takes place in the intersection of three agencies—the teacher, the learner, and the knowledge they together produce" (p. 3). Bok (2006) argues that there is a universalized norm of "neglecting" pedagogy in contemporary higher education. He attributes this in part to the idea that *pedagogy* is, by its definition, *both the art and the science* of teaching. This neglect is reflected in the gap between the significant increase in research about learning and student outcomes in postsecondary education and the sustained and implicit belief that teaching is intuitive and cannot be taught (Lee, Poch, Williams, & Shaw, 2012). A friend of Amy's in a writing studies department was encouraged by senior colleagues *not to conduct pedagogical research* because it wasn't "rigorous" and it wasn't "really research." This is a surprising regression in a department that does the work of a field historically organized around the value of teaching and learning writing development, but not surprising in current contexts of higher education. However, it is also not uncommon. "Even in research on education, pedagogy is often an elusive element," so that "within journals focused on college teaching, little research or theory focuses on pedagogy or learning environment factors effective across cultural identities and norms" (Chavez, 2010, p. 54).

Who We Are

As scholars and teachers, we have come to intercultural pedagogy from diverse disciplinary and experiential backgrounds. Amy Lee came to this project from a specific discipline (humanities) and field of origin (composition/writing studies), and enters the conversation from a specific conceptual framework (feminist and critical pedagogy). Mary Katherine O'Brien entered this work from the fields of international education and intercultural theory and from her work as an international student adviser and faculty development trainer. Bob Poch and Catherine Solheim, historian and family scientist respectively, bring different research and disciplinary training, as well as a range and depth of experience in undergraduate classrooms and graduate education, as well as community-based, field-based, and international teaching. In writing this book together, we seek to integrate research on pedagogy and practice/experience with pedagogy. What brought us into collaboration was our shared investment in improving support for teachers and students in higher education classrooms, particularly around engaging diversity. Our goal is to support the development, confidence, and capacity of faculty to operate within the complex system of a classroom environment in ways that help diverse members thrive and in ways that support the engagement of diversity as a resource.

Amy and Bob have focused extensively on critical and culturally responsive pedagogy, working with faculty, students, and extant research in their disciplines of origin and across disciplines. Over the years of our work and respective collaboration, we, and the practitioners in the fields most invested in this work, have thought a lot about what to call this work. Critical pedagogy? Culturally relevant pedagogy? Signature pedagogy? Equity pedagogy? Embodied pedagogy? Intercultural pedagogy? Multicultural pedagogy? Engaging diversity? The qualifier one chooses to put in front of "pedagogy" is a heavy signifier; it signals something about one's location within a particular historical context, field of study, and a sociopolitical lens. For this project, we have settled on the term *intercultural pedagogy*. We have done so with deep intention because the term makes explicit both vectors of the equation, intercultural and pedagogy. We will orient our readers to this term in both its constituent parts and its synergistic whole.

How This Book Is Organized and Why

This book provides scholar-practitioners with a theoretical foundation, practical tools, and an iterative process for designing, implementing, and continually refining a pedagogy that supports diverse students and intercultural outcomes. The volume is organized into sections to support the iterative cycle of knowledge acquisition and awareness development, design and implementation, and reflection/revision that is characteristic of critical pedagogies as well as of intercultural development models.

Developing awareness about assumptions, ideas, and habits we have formed as teachers and reflecting on how/whether our established habits support intercultural pedagogy intercultural and equity goals are the first steps toward intercultural pedagogy. We resonate to the idea of a "stepwise" approach (a concept borrowed from Katila, Merilainen, & Tienarirefer [2010], in their inclusion work): a sequence of questioning, reflecting, assessing, and refining in order to support knowledge, reflective capacity, and practices that contribute to intercultural pedagogy. As they described,

> First, we need to be able to describe and account for current practices. . . .
> Second, we need to be prepared to ask questions about the status quo;
> the taken-for granted practices it sustains and the knowledge it privileges.
> Third, and only then, we are ready to offer constructive alternatives and
> provide suggestions for change. In other words, we must be prepared to
> move from constitutive questions (what? how?) via critical and evaluative questions (how good is it?) to constructive questions (how could it be
> otherwise?). (Katila et al., 2010, p. 7)

This book is organized to take a stepwise approach, moving from inquiry on normative institutional practices and the shaping of situated, individual practice (*what is it?*) to assessment (*how well does it work?*) and revision (*how else could we do it?*). Chapter 2 identifies some of the normative institutional values and practices that often discount teaching and reflective pedagogical practices, and further defines the meaning and values of *intercultural pedagogy*. Chapters 3 through 6 include insights into the reflective practice we have engaged as teachers as well as the pedagogical revisions that emerged from those reflections and provide invitations for you to review and reflect on your development as a teacher and your course design, activities, and classroom environment.

We are interested in not merely the pedagogy argued for but the pedagogy of our argument (Gore, 1992). Hence, we have tried to shape a book that breathes life into the ideas through its organization, structure, and the choices we made about including different perspectives and modes of writing. Author team members have each come from different disciplines, generations, and institutional contexts, and we have sought to explicitly highlight and engage that diversity throughout the book. We have first-person reflections, classroom activities, and annotated assignments that illustrate the dynamic process of intention, experiment/implement, critique, and refinement that characterize pedagogy and intercultural interaction. Each section invites you to reflect on and reframe the ways in which your pedagogy supports or sustains your field, discipline, and/or the goals of critical intercultural pedagogy. You will find case studies that can serve as illustrations of how we have adapted our teaching to align with our emerging intercultural pedagogy. You will find questions, activities, and exercises that will actively engage you in reflection, revision, and/or action.

We hope that you will use the book as it best supports you; we imagine you might use it in different ways over time as you develop your intercultural pedagogy. The book can be used by individuals or by communities of practitioners using the book together, whether your community is a graduate class of future practitioners, a department, or colleagues brought together by an affinity area of common need or interest. If you do not have immediate access to a community of practice, it is our hope that the guiding questions in this volume give you opportunities to engage and, perhaps, form the basis of a way of connecting with colleagues who share similar interests and values. In our own experiences of reflecting on some of the key moments that have influenced our development, the four of us identified moments of collective engagement as absolutely essential to our growth. Whether Catherine's experience as a fellow in an international teaching and learning cohort working with Mary Katherine, Bob's experience in an interdisciplinary team teaching experience, or Amy's experience of engaging in collaborative active research with her undergraduates, each of us points to those experiences as challenging, nurturing, and spurring our inquiry as we experimented and ultimately developed our respective intercultural pedagogy.

2

UNLEARNING TEACHING

A Framework for Intercultural Pedagogy

> The classroom remains the most radical space of possibility in the academy. . . . I celebrate teaching that enables transgressions—a movement against and beyond boundaries. It is that movement which makes education the practice of freedom. (hooks, 1994, p. 12)

Intercultural pedagogy often pushes against or disrupts deeply rooted institutional norms of teaching, learning, disciplinary thinking, and assessment. In this chapter, we define *intercultural pedagogy*, we present core tenets that intercultural pedagogy disrupts, and we offer counter values that work to support it. We speak here and in following chapters about disruption as positive action that strengthens our pedagogy through intentional processes of revision—of re-visioning our interactions with students and our conceptions about our disciplines and fields, the structure of our courses, and the ways in which we assess learning. We begin with defining what we mean by *intercultural pedagogy*.

Defining *Intercultural Pedagogy*

In thinking about the complex factors leading to the American Civil War, historian Edward Ayers (2005) cautioned, "We should simply refuse to settle for simple explanations for complex problems" (p. 143). Ayers reminds us that what distinguishes a *scholarly* approach to something, what characterizes research across disciplines, fields, epochs, and texts, is the refusal to simplify what we *know* to be complex. This is true of pedagogical and intercultural relationships as well. They are simply not simple. Intercultural pedagogy, like its constitutive components (intercultural *and* pedagogy), doesn't just occur naturally or inevitably. It requires intention.

Intentionality includes clarity about what we mean by intercultural pedagogy so that it guides our decisions and practices. By intercultural, we refer to all the forms of human diversity, social group and individual, visible or invisible, that define *cultural identity* as perceived, imposed, or self-defined. More than that, we use *intercultural* to make explicit the incontestable reality that these forms of human diversity not only come into contact with one another in a classroom but also *impact* one another. Therefore, in choosing to use the term *inter*cultural, we refer not only to the presence but also to the interdependence of forms of human diversity within a classroom. Whether intentional or not, whether visible or not, whether orchestrated or not, or whether a collision or a coming together, interactions among forms of human diversity are unavoidable in social and institutional arenas, such as classrooms.

In a largely parallel manner that recognizes the deeper learning possibilities that student diversity can create, Simon (1988) clarifies the meaning of pedagogy in relationship to teaching:

> "Pedagogy" is a more complex and extensive term than "teaching," referring to the integration in practice of particular curriculum content and design, classroom strategies and techniques, a time and space for the practice of those strategies and techniques, and evaluation purposes and methods. . . . In other words, talk about pedagogy is simultaneously talk about the details of what students and others might do together and the cultural politics such practices support. (p. 371)

Simon's definition draws out several critical aspects of pedagogy. It is relational to the individuals involved and to moments in time and space informed by fields of play that are not static. Pedagogy is also an *integrative* activity, not an application. It involves attention to the reciprocal nature of learning environments and to the interdependence among what is being studied, who is participating, and how the interactions are being designed and supported. By definition, *pedagogy* explicitly connects theory and practice, reflection and action, and the essential, inevitable elements of any teaching-learning interaction (who, what, and how of teaching and learning).

In joining the signifiers *intercultural* and *pedagogy*, we draw on and modify the assumptions that form Kim's (2005) matrix of interethnic communications to flesh out a concept of intercultural learning environments:

1. Intercultural learning environments happen whenever a member of a classroom (teacher or students) sees self, subject matter, or other participants in light of his or her respective identity/ethnicity.

2. Intercultural learning environments inevitably involve context—the current situation, the environment, and the historical associations/learned ways of being or knowing in that situation or environment.

3. Intercultural learning environments are "open systems" whose components (situation, environment, and communicator) are functionally and conceptually interdependent.

We want to emphasize that you are teaching in and experiencing intercultural classrooms *regardless of whether* you want to, *whether* you are aware of it, and *whether* you think it is your responsibility or relevant to your discipline. It isn't a choice, because *human diversity* (as defined earlier) is present in every classroom, regardless of whether it is visible and whether it is solicited. That said, the mere presence of demographic and social difference in a given environment does not guarantee a supportive intercultural environment, nor does it guarantee that participants will deepen or develop effective intercultural skills, habits, or awareness (Harari, 1992; Leask, 2009; Mestenhauser, 2011). Just as the presence of diversity does not in and of itself result in equity, inclusion, or the development of intercultural effectiveness, an institutional desire to prioritize "diversity" or to state a valuing of student and faculty capacity to effectively engage diversity does not translate into faculty and students actually being able to engage diversity. The findings of Dey, Ott, Antonaros, Barnhardt, and Holsapple (2010) were typical of other multi-institutional studies, concluding that "while higher education places high value on engaging diverse perspectives, [institutions] need to do much more to ensure that . . . students actually develop these capacities across several years in college" (p. ix).

Therefore, drawing on the concepts of intercultural and pedagogy, we define *intercultural pedagogy* as the commitment (not just the desire) to make intentional, informed decisions that enable our courses to engage and support diversity and inclusion. Teachers must be willing to develop the capacity to do that and commit to continuously reflecting on for whom and to what extent course design, activities, and instruction are achieving these outcomes (Lee et al., 2012).

The complexity of intercultural pedagogy and the dynamic diverse environments in which it is used makes necessary the use of an equally complex literature to gain insight into how intercultural pedagogy can be used effectively within institutions, disciplines, and fields where such pedagogy appears foreign, irrelevant, and disconnected. Throughout this book, we draw on scholarship from a range of relevant fields of study, including those that explore specific disciplinary values, Western academic culture, non-Western epistemologies, critical pedagogy, and intercultural development theory.

Although the "fields" of scholarship we engage are highly diverse and seemingly disconnected, they are unified in a critical appraisal of teaching and learning in systems of higher education that cling to long-standing structures that maintain the cultural dominance of one group over diverse others. A multidisciplinary approach enabled us to see possibilities for facilitating effective participatory learning within classrooms of culturally diverse students. For example, we discovered that revisions to the structure and pedagogy within a freshman-level U.S. history course were informed by the scholarship of nonhistorians, such as bell hooks, Laura Rendón, Paulo Freire, and Vine Deloria. Although their ideas do not appear in the disciplinary literature of history (and probably not in the literature of many other disciplines or fields), they have much to offer in terms of how history (or other courses) can be taught effectively within contemporary classrooms filled with culturally diverse students. There is power and possibility in combining our discipline-based literature with the literature pertaining to intercultural pedagogy. Therefore, we posit that we must seek interdisciplinary perspectives upon which to build our intercultural pedagogy.

Intercultural Pedagogy Requires Disruption

Even a cursory review of the multidisciplinary literature we have drawn on throughout this book will uncover a consistent theme: the need to disrupt the status quo so that all students have better opportunities to learn in ways that reflect, utilize, and value who they are. Scholars who write about different facets of intercultural pedagogy illuminate acts of disruption or the need to confront existing practices. bell hooks (1994) speaks of the need to "transgress" engrained conceptions of teaching that remove faculty and students from meaningful and joyful encounters with learning; Paulo Freire (1970) writes about the struggle and ongoing tension between oppression and liberation in education; Michael Apple (2015) documents the persistent relationships between knowledge and power that produce socially unjust outcomes; and Vine Deloria and Daniel Wildcat (2001) recount the historically rooted but still contemporary "crisis in education" as schools and colleges actively dishonor indigenous ways of knowing while privileging Western ways. Each of these scholars identified important societal and institutional factors that have worked their way into educational settings in ways that harm relationships between teachers and students, disconnect teaching and learning, and fail to utilize and value diversity. Other challenging factors, such as quiet apathy toward change, ready acceptance of current practices, and uncritical compliance with time-honored disciplinary-related norms, are more subtle and harder to detect, yet work against engaging intercultural pedagogy. For example, many scholars of teaching and learning have examined daily habits, enforced by institutional and disciplinary norms, that sanction a lack of consciousness that may characterize our teaching and our induction of new teachers. Rendón (2009) theorized about the power and depth of what she termed *agreements*, defined as assumptions and beliefs that we might uncritically adopt through socialization into the values and priorities of our discipline, department, and institution. Given historical inequities and lack of inclusion in academic fields and spaces, these unexamined agreements may perpetuate traditions and habits of mind and teaching that do not support intercultural pedagogy. Briefly, we describe *some* of the most prevalent practices and norms that intercultural pedagogy must challenge and disrupt if we are to design and implement our courses and meaningfully assess intended learner outcomes in ways that engage and support diversity and inclusion.

"Mindless" uncritical acceptance of current teaching and learning practices. Langer (1997) examined the habit of "mindlessness." Mindful versus mindless is a way of naming what is intentional versus what is unconscious or invisible, a way of making explicit what may be implicit. Mindlessness is the "heavy reliance on familiar frames of reference, old routinized designs, or categories and customary ways of doing things" (Ting-Toomey, 2005, p. 226). Finnish scholars Katila and colleagues (2010) use a similarly powerful concept of habituated modes of perception or practice, "agreements" to account for the continuation of hegemony in relation to inclusion/ equity in higher education. The institution or discipline incentivizes us to act in accordance with our unexamined agreements, which are *not* those that privilege diversity, pedagogy, or intercultural effectiveness. Thus the system acculturates or "seduces us into compliance not by direct force but by consent" (Katila et al., 2010, p. 4). Collins (1997) refers to this system of higher education as one that is "closed" and wherein "those of us who are insiders to that system go about our business, occasionally surprised by a tacit ground rule we hadn't yet internalized, but for the most part we have been quietly socialized by extended stays in college, then graduate school, to norms we cannot name" (p. 79). In essence, we must unlearn mindless practices and norms of institutional socialization, including those that relate to teaching.

In an article published by *College English*, Shari Stenberg and Amy Lee (2002) posed the following scenario:

> You arrive at graduate school in time for the three-day orientation, which consists of a series of workshops "training" you to be a scholar. One half-day session covers the conference proposal and presentation; another trains new students to write seminar papers; a third focuses on the prospectus and dissertation; yet another teaches the composition of articles for refereed journals. At the end of three days, you are ostensibly "trained" in the

basics required to contribute to your profession as a scholar and researcher. While you might continue to develop these "skills" as you advance through courses, exams, dissertations, and professional forums, your program can rest assured that it has done its duty by you, having covered the fundamentals and thereby "orienting" you. (p. 326)

Obviously, no doctoral program would presume scholars or researchers could develop to a level of professional readiness this way. And yet, that is a habituated model for teacher preparation/induction in higher education. The scenario is intended to provoke reflection on the absurd oversimplification of pedagogy that is systemic in our doctoral programs and institutions.

What has changed a decade and a half later? Certainly, there is more rhetorical attention to the importance of "good" teaching and to the presence of (and often the "challenge" of) diverse students. We hear more talk about active learning, student engagement, academic technologies, and "internationalizing" the curriculum. But our impression is that much of this attention is underscored by efficiency and economics more than equity. We don't see this rhetorical attention translating into institutionalized practices, including resource allocation, or doctoral or promotion/tenure requirements. Centers for "teaching and learning" have closed, merged, gone "online," and become centers for "educational innovation," a discursive marker of the emphasis being on research and not on the people or process of teaching and learning.

Disciplinary foci that encourage a stronger relationship with the subject matter than with students. Disciplinarity remains the foundational organizational schema for higher education and the basis for credentialing and expertise. Bodies of knowledge take precedence over activities of engaging knowledge with others. Embedded in this model are core assumptions that deeply inform the way we value, understand, and implement teacher preparation (Stenberg & Lee, 2002). Most important to our purposes are the following: (a) the professor's primary relationship is with the discipline, not with the students; (b) expertise in the classroom is grounded in the mastery of a subject matter and not in learning theory, intercultural effectiveness, or pedagogy; (c) this is fundamentally an *acquisition* versus a *developmental* model. One "picks up" the basics of teaching through watching other teachers or by participating in workshops or trainings when required or as "needed."

We recognize that teachers often need a "just in time" resource, and those should be available and well-informed. The desire for concrete, immediate, and proven practices and tools is understandable and not, in and of itself, a problem. That said, the initial impulse to "try some things" or to "fix some things" or to "deal with some things" in our classrooms must be a *starting* point and not a long-term solution or conclusion. "Fixing" something or "plugging something in" will mire you between deficit-based and supplemental approaches, the former conceptualized as someone's "lack" needing attention, and the latter characterized by tacking on intercultural and pedagogical elements to an existing course.

This habitual focus on practical matters is normative, and therefore often unexamined and habitual rather than strategic and purposeful. Referring to a dominant practitioner-focused approach to teaching and learning in composition studies, Stephen North (1987) described it as focused on *what* to do "as a means to an end determined by someone else, imposed from outside, beyond the bounds of the teacher's immediate relationship with the students" (as cited in Horner & Lu, 1999, p. 21). Practitioners are concerned with what has worked, is working, or might work but not necessarily with *why*. North (1987) wrote, "This bedrock pragmatism is habit-forming. Practitioners tend to become habitually impatient with complicated causal analyses, which in turn makes them relatively cavalier about such analyses, even for the purposes of inquiry" (as cited in Horner & Lu, 1999, p. 21).

Institutional devaluing of learning to teach. The process of learning to teach remains undervalued, disengaged by, and largely invisible within institutions of higher education in their preparation of future faculty as well as in their support for and commitment to continued development of current faculty. We saw this not only across institutions but also reflected in the journals and conference programming of professional associations. By and large, teaching is not enfranchised, intellectualized, valued, prioritized, or meaningfully assessed. Without some level of formal, systematic inclusion and assessment, teaching remains a sidebar to everything else.

This dynamic also applies to the meaningful, substantive inclusion of diversity, intercultural competency, or applied multicultural theory. Institutions and disciplines have not opted, by and large, to organize themselves around diversity, inclusion, or intercultural effectiveness. Historically, disciplines and institutions have "taken on" or "taken up" multiculturalism or diversity theory when need presents itself, such as recruiting/retaining more diverse students and meeting employer demands for more "diversity" skills. This is a gross oversimplification of many specific initiatives and sites, but if one takes a broad stroke, this is not so off the mark.

Perpetuating inequality within classrooms. In the absence of critical attention to diversity and intercultural development and an enactment of the status quo, the classroom can reinforce inequity and the perpetuation of dominant culture perspectives. Exclusion and inequity are built into the normative/traditional curriculum and instruction in contemporary education. As Apple (2015) argued, rather than simply asking whether students have mastered a particular subject matter and have done well on our all too common tests, we should ask a different set of questions: Whose knowledge is this? How did it become "official"? What is the relationship between this knowledge and who has cultural, social, and economic capital in this society? Who benefits from these definitions of legitimate knowledge and who does not? What can we do as critical educators and activists to change existing educational and social inequalities and to create curricula and teaching that are more socially just? (p. 188)

Numerous scholars echo Apple's observations. Rendón's (2009) "agreement of monoculturalism" (p. 41) identifies the pervasive privileging and valuing of Western epistemologies over those of non-Western peoples, including those of indigenous people. Deloria and Wildcat (2001) concur, noting,

Education in the English-American context resembles indoctrination more than it does other forms of teaching because it insists on implanting a particular body of knowledge and a specific view of the world, which often does not correspond to the life experiences that people have or might be expected to encounter. (p. 42)

Betty Leask (2009) writes about *the hidden curriculum*, which she defines as

incidental lessons that are learned about power and authority, what and whose knowledge is valued and what and whose knowledge is not valued, from such things as which textbook and references are used and the way that in-class and out-of-class activities are organized. (p. 207)

The hidden curriculum is, of course, always present, and not just on display in educational exchange. It is what differentiates those who implicitly know the rules for success from those who struggle to adapt to a given educational environment.

Invitation for Reflection

1. *What "agreements" are present in my teaching? Which agreements are intentional, and which reflect assumptions I have not yet questioned?*
2. *Where am I "stuck" in habitual ways of thinking that get in the way of creating an inclusive environment?*
3. *Do I have habitual ways of thinking that may be unconsciously "agreeing" with or perpetuating inequities?*

4. *How can I challenge my students to move out of habitual ways of think-ing about difference so as to support their intercultural competence/cognitive complexity?*

Intercultural Pedagogy Requires New Agreements and Explicit Values

The reality is that any of us who teaches is working according to some version of pedagogy and is also communicating something about intercultural com-munication and the value of diversity in *every course* we teach, regardless of whether inherited, intentional, or productive. Throughout this chapter, we have sought to uncover the ways that mindless pedagogy is cultivated and to argue that intercultural pedagogy requires a deliberate decision and requisite actions to resist and to counter mindless teaching. If mindless pedagogy is characterized by an unexamined reliance on routines, and practitioner-based pedagogy focused on the "what works" not the "why," what habits of mind and action characterize intercultural pedagogy? What values and agreements are present? What internal and external values and agreements are in tension with intercultural pedagogy and need to be recast?

To respond to those questions, we articulate some of the core agreements that we argue must characterize intercultural pedagogy. Although these are "agreements" as Rendón (2009) conceptualizes them, we have chosen to identify them as core *values* of intercultural pedagogy. To value something is a mind-set, an intention—a decision to agree. In a sense, values embody agreements—that is, to value assumes that we agree and are committed to act. Values inform our lived experience, our day-to-day practice and our choices of action. Referring to values rather than tenets or principles helps us communicate explicitly that intercultural pedagogy has an experiential, lived, practical dimension as well as a theoretical one. As we briefly describe each value ahead, we infuse within them the scholarship of others who underscore and further expand on the central ideas embedded within the values.

Value 1: Intercultural Pedagogy Pursues Equity and Inclusion in Classrooms

Classrooms have the potential to be particularly powerful spaces to engage diversity and intercultural development when faculty, course content, and pedagogy are considered in conjunction with the compositional diversity of the students (Milem, Chang, & Antonio, 2005). In contemporary public life in the United States, classrooms are among the few spaces in which diverse groups predictably come together in pursuit of a common agenda (complet-ing a course). As Lee and colleagues (2012) wrote, students from varied backgrounds and social groups are drawn to common courses, the classroom is a unique space where patterns of segregation and poor communication found on the outside can be powerfully interrupted. Classrooms are natural environments where students gain knowledge about diversity, but also arenas of practice where they can develop, apply, reflect on and refine the skills that are necessary to respectful and purposeful collaborations across difference. (p. 8)

In order to realize this potential, we need to shift from a content-focused paradigm to a pedagogy that supports intercultural development and communication. We need teachers who can effectively facilitate respectful interactions that develop students' intercultural skills.

Intercultural pedagogy acknowledges the historical reality that privilege, status, and authority have categorically conferred upon some categories of human difference and denied systematically to others; this reality is reflected in the dynamics of any public space. Whether you examine statistics related to persistence to degree and graduation or surveys on climate, engagement, and satisfaction, data point to these realities in institutions of higher education.

Pursuing equity and inclusion requires an active acknowledgment of the systemic, historical inequity in access and support for diverse learners. It identifies the need for institutions to move beyond intention to action that improves their capacity to recognize and challenge inequity and to support and engage diversity. However, awareness and the sense of urgency toward this end vary greatly across colleagues and their respective disciplines. We hear that some disciplines acculturate their members to think of inclusion, equity, and diversity as "separate from" the disciplinary endeavor. Other disciplines acculturate members to think of themselves as "highly intercultural" by nature of their disciplinary content, although training in skills, practices, or interactive techniques (and not content/knowledge) is fundamentally absent outside of research methodologies.

Therefore, a committed intercultural pedagogy is proactive, rather than reactive or transactional in matters of diversity and equity. If we are not actively engaging diversity, then we are actively disengaging it. Intercultural pedagogy doesn't just occur naturally or inevitably. The research is clear that *intercultural* development is a longitudinal process, taking place over time and involving cognitive, intrapersonal, interpersonal, and environmental factors. Intercultural *pedagogy* doesn't just happen either; equity and inclusion don't "naturally" result from the presence of demographic diversity. Most of us didn't become effective teachers just because we meant well by students and knew our discipline. We reiterate that it requires intention; reflection; assessment; and, we will argue, a community of practitioners to support, challenge, critique, and prompt one another, whether the community is in the form of a classroom, an online professional group, or a group of colleagues.

Value 2: Intercultural Pedagogy Recognizes That Expertise Is Fluid and Developmental

Intercultural pedagogy is not something one finally masters or "knows" or becomes an expert at doing. It is a lifelong journey that reflects a theoretical understanding that effective teaching and intercultural effectiveness (and hence intercultural pedagogy) are developmental processes (J. M. Bennett, 2009; M. J. Bennett, 1993; Deardorff, 2006). We can gain skills, knowledge, experience, and confidence, but we are on a lifelong journey and will never "master" it. In part, this is true of so many aspects of our teaching and broader educational environment. We are continually in flux, always encountering new influences, factors, and elements in teaching. It is also because intercultural pedagogy is in-relation-to the students, the subject matter, the physical or virtual classroom environments, and factors that influence and impact our teaching and students' learning. Bok (2006) described pedagogy as an art and a science; we might describe intercultural pedagogy as a process *and* a product.

A component of this value is that it is impossible for faculty to support students' intercultural development if faculty are not developing their own intercultural experiences, skills, knowledge, and awareness (Sanderson, 2008). Just as we would not expect an anatomy teacher to automatically be an effective algebra teacher or communications teacher, we don't expect every faculty member to immediately be effective at supporting development of students' intercultural skills. A good analogy might be the writing across the curriculum models wherein writing instruction is best supported through a multimodal approach; it is led by those who specialize in that discipline and involves faculty *across the curriculum* rather than being the sole responsibility of faculty in writing/composition studies. This dual model of supporting depth of expertise (by having a writing program/department) along with distributed expertise and responsibility for writing requires investment in faculty across the curriculum in the form of training, development, feedback, and mentoring to enable them to support students' writing. So we advocate for an *intercultural development* across the curriculum theory and model, which we seek to advance here.

Intentional intercultural pedagogy often requires sitting with the discomfort of not knowing whether we have encountered a difference that makes a difference and how to proceed in a way that is respectful and intentional. The dynamics that arise in an intercultural classroom can be particularly difficult to navigate because they are rooted in aspects of identity, history, power, and privilege that may be unfamiliar to us and which we may not know how to explore with our peers or our students. We can even be fairly knowledgeable about these dynamics, whether personally or in the abstract, and still struggle to interact with others in a way that feels interculturally or interpersonally effective. As J. M. Bennett (2009) pointed out, "In fact, cultural knowledge does not equal intercultural competence since a person can be an expert on a particular aspect of Chinese culture and yet be unable to negotiate with his Chinese counterparts" (p. 123).

Intercultural pedagogy might be understood as developing a mind-set of comfort with *not* knowing rather than comfort based on expertise. This is one of the disruptive factors within intercultural pedagogy as it intersects with oneself and the academy—the ability to be at ease with not knowing when intellectual competency so often focuses on knowing. Intercultural pedagogy integrates this "not knowing" as humility.

Cultural humility is understood as critical to intercultural development. Hook, Davis, Owen, Worthington, and Utsey (2013) define *cultural humility* as "an interpersonal stance that is other-oriented, or open to the other, in relation to aspects of cultural identity that are most important to the [person]" (p. 354). This represents one mind-set that may help us to move away from seeking competence into a process-oriented approach to knowing others. The call for cultural humility asks us to first suspend *our* evaluation of situations and people based on our previous knowledge and then requires us to work *with them* to understand what they see as the most important aspects of their cultural identity in a given situation. The *inter*cultural is thus based in these *inter*actions, moving beyond our perceptions of culture as something to be learned or understood.

If cultural humility is critical to intercultural development, we would argue that pedagogical humility is critical to intercultural pedagogy. Patricia Cranton's (2001) definition of an *authentic teacher* is helpful as we consider the idea of pedagogical humility. She wrote that an authentic teacher (an intercultural teacher in our context) is one who "understands who she is as a teacher, works well and clearly with her own style, and continues to reflect on her practice, grow, and develop" (Cranton, 2001, p. 36). She asserts the importance of a process for this work, continuing: "we each, individually, find our own place within these perspectives through questioning, contemplation, and reflection on our basic nature, preferences, experience, and values" (Cranton, 2001, p. 41). Sanderson (2009) further explored the task of translating self-awareness into teaching practice. He asserted that "it is important to know that the ideal is not an end point. There is a need for ongoing awareness through lifelong learning to continually reinvigorate ourselves, regardless of our competence at a particular point in time" (Sanderson, 2009, p. 8).

It must be acknowledged that a stance of pedagogical humility represents a tremendous paradigm shift for teaching and learning; it runs contrary to the way that most of us have been academically trained at nearly all levels of schooling. Even in learning environments where educators assume the role of facilitator, there is a persistent expectation that the teacher has deep subject-level knowledge to impart to students who will eventually be able to mirror back that knowledge as it was taught to them. Particularly in the context of research-extensive higher education in which we work, many of our colleagues are identified (and identify) as internationally recognized experts in a given subject area. It is, therefore, much easier to talk about "unlearning" what we know than it is to truly operate from a position of not knowing.

Value 3: Intercultural Pedagogy Relies On and Fosters Reflection and Revision

Scholars of transformative learning have long advocated the power of reflection. Reflection "allows—indeed asks—teachers (and, we would add, learners) to question their understandings, rethink their assumptions, and consider their options" (Russo & Ford, 2006, p. 3). Stopping to assess how or why we have interpreted, thought, felt, or behaved is an act of making meaning that helps us to differentiate between what we already know and what we lack frameworks to understand (Mezirow, 1990). Reflection can help us to chart a course ahead, in part by looking into the past to understand our reactions in a given context, and thinking about how we might act another time. It is an exploration of what works and what doesn't work, why, what we can and cannot change, and how to evaluate our surroundings. The more we intentionally engage in this type of reflection, the more facile we become at it; even the exploration itself is at times difficult and challenging.

Reflective capacity is understood to be critical to intercultural or multicultural effectiveness (Eisenchlas & Trevaskes, 2003; Fantini, 2009; Sanderson, 2008), and therefore we argue that it is critical to an intercultural pedagogy because it supports an individual's capacity to consider multiple perspectives, to tolerate ambiguity, to engage complexity and openness. These capacities might be considered as individuals' ability to engage in revision—of what they thought they knew, of how they thought they knew it, and of their belief that they "know" or understand others.

Revision has been a key conceptual thread across Amy's research and teaching and one she has found useful to developing teachers in higher education in her workshops and courses. As a composition scholar and teacher, Amy encountered the term *revision* frequently—at teacher training and development workshops in the writing program where she taught;

throughout the scholarship on teaching writing; in the writing process model. In those contexts, the idea of revision was generally concrete and applied: revision was an essential and specific phase of the writing process. In and out of writing classrooms, we are familiar with the idea or process of revision, but sometimes we tend to think of it as "editing" or "cleaning." Revision, however, is a substantive and complex action. In a revision stage, writers (or knowers) are deepening their intellectual grasp of their ideas, and argument or message, coming to a more developed and nuanced understanding of their purpose and audience/cocommunicators. In the revision stage, we begin to shape the form of our knowledge (organization, voice, diction, tone, sequencing of ideas, language choices) to more strategically shape the form in ways that are strategic and effective for the purpose and intended audience, refining the organization, elaborating on the ideas, and attuning the voice or perspective.

To re-vision is to re-see. Quite literally, it is "to vision again." Re-vision is critical to intercultural and pedagogical relationships because it names the capacity to employ multiple lenses in thoughtful reflection; mindful sight, we might call it. It acknowledges limits of visibility and seeks to discover that which is invisible. Reflective revision allows us to draw wisdom from what has been lived and to develop mindful sight to guide us forward.

Invitation for Reflection

1. *In what ways are reflection, revision, and humility enacted or applied in my pedagogy?*
2. *If they're not, how can I meaningfully apply them within my pedagogy?*
3. *What value do they, or will they, bring?*

Conclusion

We conclude this chapter by reiterating the core values we believe are essential to developing an intercultural pedagogy: learning to be intercultural is developmental rather than something to be acquired; ambiguity and complexity are critical to engaging equity and diversity; and mindfulness and revision are essential and at times uncomfortable reflexive actions. These three values are drawn from literatures in multicultural education, intercultural development, and the scholarship of teaching and learning, all of which cohere around fundamental principles.

The three core values discussed in this chapter can be applied to learners as well as teachers. In other words, although we focus this book on teacher development and discuss why these values are critical to your development of intercultural pedagogy, we also note that your course design and implementation should seek to support your students' enactment of these values.

Before moving on to the next chapter, we invite you to revisit your responses to earlier reflection questions, "revise" those responses if your ideas have developed since then, and consider the following questions as you begin to shape your intercultural pedagogy.

- *How do I define* intercultural pedagogy?
- *In what ways am I willing to commit to developing an intercultural pedagogy?*
- *What investments of time and energy am I willing to make?*
- *What benefits will the development and enactment of an intercultural pedagogy have for my teaching? For my students' learning?*

The next chapter outlines the authors' journeys to developing their intercultural pedagogy. They represent different disciplines, different starting points, and different developmental trajectories to where they now enact their evolving intercultural pedagogies. We invite you to begin your journey as you read and reflect about theirs.

3

LEARNING TO TEACH
INTERCULTURALLY

Reflection is a more deliberate process that allows—indeed asks—teachers
to question their understandings, rethink their assumptions, and consider
their options. (Russo & Ford, 2006, p. 6)

In chapter 1 we stated our intention to focus in this volume on the *teacher*
in Lusted's (1986) triad of pedagogy. In that spirit, this chapter examines the
"Self as teacher, teacher as Self" (Cranton, 2001, p. 43), acknowledging the
complexity of "self" and the many identities that may entail. Specifically,
we turn here to the act of reflection and its role in the development of an
intercultural pedagogy.

Critical self-reflection is key in our development as intercultural teachers, as individuals who teach in diverse classrooms, who honor and integrate
a variety of perspectives into classroom discourse, and who embrace the dissonance and discomfort that support growth in our students and ourselves.
Reflection on critical moments of our lived experience—in or out of the
classroom—reveals developing the skills, capacities, and awareness that are
at the core of intercultural pedagogy; we developed them over time and
with mishaps and regression, not in a linear or acquisitional way. Critical
moments shaped our conceptions and understanding of intercultural and
pedagogical identity, and, subsequently, our understanding and implementation of intercultural pedagogy.

There is a breadth of literature that supports these claims, in the scholarship both on transformative learning (e.g., Cranton, 2006; Dirkx, 1998;
Mezirow, 1997) and on intercultural development (e.g., Fantini, 2009; Kim,
2009; Sanderson, 2008). We have chosen to touch briefly on those sources
here, but to devote the majority of this chapter to critical self-reflections
from authors Bob and Catherine, who in the process of writing this book
explored the relationships among their early life experiences, scholarly

influences, and critical shifts in teaching and learning. We have heard from colleagues, anecdotally and formally, that examples of the processes we are advocating in this book are often not shared or readily available; therefore, these reflections are offered as illustrations of that work and as models for cultural and pedagogical self-inventories. (Catherine commented recently, in fact, that the written reflections supported her in making key connections between early life and career experiences with her current pedagogical intentions.) This chapter concludes with guiding questions, similar to those Bob and Catherine used, that may help you to engage in this process yourself.

Foundations for Reflection

Critical self-reflection on our backgrounds, identities, and assumptions helps us to make meaning of how we present in interactions with diverse others and as facilitators of learning; to assess how or why we have interpreted, thought, felt, or behaved. Reflection as an act of making meaning is a central tenet in the literature of transformative learning (Cranton, 2006; Dirkx, 1998; Mezirow, 1997). Reckoning back to the discussion of humility in chapter 2, reflection is also a way of identifying what we do not know and lack frameworks for understanding.

Among scholars of intercultural development, there is nearly universal agreement (in a field based on the premise that there are few universals, no less) that self-awareness is an essential step in the ongoing and dynamic process of developing interculturally (Sanderson, 2008). Critical self-awareness, or a deeper understanding of what shapes our own behavior, attitudes, and impulses, helps us develop a framework to better interpret and inform our interactions with others (Eisenchlas & Trevaskes, 2003). It may seem paradoxical that to "know" others better, we must first know ourselves, yet self-awareness and self-understanding are often facilitated by our interactions with the others we are trying to understand, and by our efforts to understand the link between background, values, worldview, and actions—for ourselves as well as for others. Freire (1970, 1973, 1998) acknowledged this when he wrote about *concientização*, a concept he simultaneously presented as awareness of selfhood and a critical look at the self in-relation-to or among others. The meaning that we make of these interactions is key to our self-understanding and the eventual way that we develop an intercultural way of being in the world. Questions for cultural self-reflection often focus, therefore, on our family of origin; the values that we were exposed to in our early lives, and how those have changed over time; critical incidents with others; experiences that prompted us to do or think of things differently;

the identities that we have held at different points in our lives; and, interpretively, the ways that these factors shape our attitudes and behaviors.

Cranton (2001) advocates for introspection and self-awareness as critical tools for teachers who want to develop intentional intercultural pedagogy that breaks "from the constraints of uncritically assimilated values, assumptions and social norms of the herd" (p. vii). She writes, "The way we make meaning out of experiences determines our habitual expectations and our habits of mind" (p. 15), calling to mind Rendón's (2009) agreements as described in chapter 2. Rendón argues that agreements are often adopted uncritically during the process of assimilating to one's field, discipline, and institutional role. She maintains that these agreements exert a strong pull and they tend to promote historically entrenched values and argues that new, intentional agreements can be formed and implemented through self-reflection guided by the following kinds of questions:

> Why have I not broken out of a belief system that is oppressive in nature for many students and faculty? How is my behavior upholding power structures in the academy? What do I believe about who can and cannot learn? How am I choosing my curriculum—what assumptions do I follow, and is the curriculum truly inclusive and multicultural in nature? If not, what prevents me from doing this and why am I going along with this limiting view of knowledge? (Rendón, 2009, pp. 135–136)

In the process of writing this book, Bob and Catherine spent time in deep reflection and wrote about how they came to their current conception of intercultural pedagogy. They grappled with Rendón's questions in this process, as well as other intercultural and pedagogical tensions. After identifying critical junctures in their stories when significant awareness or learning occurred, we present them as examples of how two different people from two different disciplines developed their cultural awareness and identity, and how that influenced their identities as teacher and scholar. Their different experiences and paths underscore that there is no lockstep process to an intercultural pedagogy. It is our hope that your consideration of the ensuing critical areas of influence will offer insights to help you shape your own intercultural pedagogy: (a) early formative experiences in developing cultural identity; (b) academic experiences and influences; and (c) pedagogical development as teacher and scholar. After each section, we encourage you to reflect and write in response to questions we pose. In ways similar to Bob and Catherine, this will help you develop your own intercultural development narrative. We believe your intentional self-examination will bring you to a greater awareness of how you have been consciously or unconsciously shaped into your current self-as-teacher/scholar, and provide time and space to consider how those insights may help your intentional process of developing an intercultural pedagogy.

Early Formative Experiences in Developing Cultural Identity

(Catherine) I grew up in a small, rural town in northern Minnesota with a population that was ethnically and racially homogeneous White, Scandinavian/Germanic. There was little opportunity to experience difference. After graduating from college, I landed in an 18-month Peace Corps–like program that was sponsored by the United States Agency for International Development (USAID) and the Thailand Ministry of Agriculture. After one month in language school in Bangkok, I spent 17 months living in rural southern Thai villages with agrarian families and working with local youth and homemaker groups. I bumped into so many differences in language, beliefs, traditions, and ways of behaving that it forced me to think about culture; not only the novel culture I was experiencing but also my own culture of origin that had shaped my beliefs, traditions, and ways of behaving.

The tensions I experienced in Thailand were critical to developing my intercultural awareness. Many fairly insignificant interactions over time pushed my awareness of differences in the ways Thais think and behave and what was "normal" to me. For example, I gained insight into the Thais' circular, relaxed view of time versus my American future-oriented linear-separable time conception. I learned that Thai watches "walk" but they "run" in America. I also learned about how I was shaped by my own culture when I became aware of my reactions to others' actions. For most of my time in Thailand, I stayed in a room and had few possessions—clothes and personal items, a guitar, a few books, a journal, a woven straw mat, a mosquito net, and a pillow. When work colleagues came into town for our monthly staff meetings, several of them stayed in my room to save money. Invariably, I'd come home and one of them was using my pillow. I remember getting really upset, actually angry, that they would dare to use my pillow without asking. I didn't want to upset things, so I rolled up my towel and used it as a pillow. But inside I was seething. As time went on, I saw that these women also freely used whatever else was in the apartment or belonged to their peers, again, without permission.

Reflecting on my strong reaction to this "violation," it began to dawn on me that a "firm boundary" I'd been taught to honor by my family had been transgressed. As one of six siblings, we were taught that we were never to use another person's things without asking first. This was a matter of respect for another's property; using without asking was disrespectful. As I thought about this, I came to realize that this was not only a family rule but also a cultural rule about individual property ownership rights, a value deeply woven into the fabric of our U.S. legal system. I had been evaluating a behavior in my new cultural context based on my own family and cultural rules. The Thai culture is more collectivist—what's mine is yours; there is little that one claims as his or her personal private property. Material things are seen as community property available to anyone who needs it. The use of my pillow was not disrespectful but rather pragmatic; the person needed a pillow and it was there.

I share these experiences and insights because I don't believe that we need a significant event or a huge epiphany to develop our awareness of difference. Rather, it is being consciously present and aware of *our* actions and reactions *and* consciously present and aware of *others'* actions and reactions in everyday experiences. We need to reflect and consider the "why" or the reason behind the "what" or the behavior or idea. We need to "check" our own cultural worldviews to be conscious of the basis for our interpretation of others' behaviors or ideas, and then we need to try to understand the behavior or idea from another perspective. Without this reflective questioning, we run the risk of interpreting behaviors or ideas from our own ethnocentrism and getting it very wrong.

(Bob) Although it probably never occurred to me as a grade-school student in the 1960s and 1970s, I lived in an ethnically diverse suburban community just across the Potomac River from Washington DC. A little more than a decade after the 1954 *Brown v. Board of Education* decision, Northern Virginia schools were becoming integrated during my elementary school years. The pace of racial integration accelerated during the mid-1970s as I progressed through high school. My classmates were a rich blend of different socioeconomic classes and ethnicities, and many of us were friends since early elementary school.

I remember learning about class differences more clearly than ethnicity, although I later saw connectivity between the two. Unlike some of my friends' fathers, my dad drove to work. He worked "downtown" in a government job that required wearing a suit and well-polished shoes. Part of our Saturday afternoon ritual was walking a few blocks to Rocky's dry-cleaning to pick up the neatly boxed shirts and three suits my dad had cleaned and pressed to wear in orderly rotation the following week. Other friends had dads who took busses to work on the Metro. Many of their fathers were heavy construction machinists and carpenters. Although they lived in neighborhoods close to my own, they were farther away by foot and were less convenient to meet after school. Unknowingly, these were early lessons in race, class, privilege, and power.

These seemingly subtle differences to teenagers were actually strong vestiges of Jim Crow communities that continued dictating population and housing patterns and economic opportunities—or their absence. Housing and jobs were largely unaltered by the first years of school integration in Virginia. Despite the presence of the U.S. Supreme Court and other branches of national government just a few miles from our homes, Washington DC, was very much a southern city in tone and history. So too was Alexandria, Virginia, where we lived.

Life within a large public high school of nearly 3,000 students was easily perceived as equal and integrative, especially given the absence of what we now call *active learning pedagogies.* The notion of equality was also perpetuated by the fact that these diverse friends were very smart and performed well academically. We sat together in an advanced comparative government class and all struggled together (and yet also separately), trying to comprehend *The Communist Manifesto* (1848). We progressed steadily and evenly through grade levels—no one in school seemed cast off or left out. Closer examination of our curriculum, books, and the pedagogy employed would have led to different conclusions. None were inclusive of the diversity of the student population or made use of diverse voices. Court decisions made the presence of diversity a reality, but the pursuit of equity and inclusion as a pedagogical commitment was sorely lacking.

It takes intentionality, awareness, and commitment to disrupt old patterns given that the weight of history seems to favor stasis. As we have argued throughout this book, a core value of intercultural pedagogy is that it pursues equity and inclusion in classrooms; and that congruence—a synchronicity between action and idea, theory and practice, value and habit—is essential in that pursuit. My learning from friends occurred mostly outside instructional spaces rather than within; I can only now imagine how many opportunities were lost by not engaging us together in class. Instruction occurred but not intercultural learning. Away from the classroom, I learned about the capacity of generous relationships among friends to transcend many class and ethnic differences; about the power of interaction in deconstructing strongly entrenched social constructions surrounding race and intellectual abilities; about the power of multicultural interactions in forming personal values and beliefs that enable productive, affirming relationships in adulthood as well as in learning spaces. I also learned through reflection about my friends how much history informs complex systems of inequality and also how institutions, such as schools, can sometimes hide inequality by denying voice, engagement, and interruptions to pedagogic uniformity and monoculturalism (Rendón, 2009). Reflecting on this reinforces how much is lost when intercultural pedagogy is not used within classrooms. Without well-informed action, the best intentions, intuitions, and content expertise will not produce intercultural pedagogy.

Pause for reflection and writing. We encourage you to take some time now to think and write about your core values and critical formative experiences that have influenced the development of those values and your cultural identity.

Invitation for Reflection

1. *What are my core values?*
2. *How (and who) contributed to the formation of those values?*
3. *How do I put them into practice today?*
4. *What are my values around education; where is the evidence of these values in my teaching?*
5. *What key life events have shaped the ways I perceive difference?*
6. *What implicit biases and stereotypes might I bring into the learning environment?*

Pedagogical Influences

(Bob) Like many others, I had no schooling or any other form of preparation to teach in diverse postsecondary classrooms. Finding guidance in a community of practitioners committed to learning about and using intercultural pedagogy has been a critical part of my development. Throughout my career that community of practitioners has taken different forms, including the scholars whose work has animated my inquiry. Among the most impactful experiences I had were the opportunity to meet historian John Hope Franklin as an undergraduate and, later, participating in a workshop led by education scholar Laura Rendón. Although I did not know it at the time, Franklin and Rendón began my process of uniting the discipline of history with intercultural pedagogy. Even though they are from different scholarly traditions, together they were exemplars of effective self-reflection and intentional action in creating equity and inclusion in diverse learning environments, which influenced me significantly.

Franklin was particularly aware of how persons experience history in highly personal ways and that personal stories have much to say about time and culture. As an African American born in rural Oklahoma in 1915, his life continually intersected with the harsh realities of Jim Crow and the protective strategies that his parents deployed to combat racist messaging and actions. Although some scholars are very detached as they write papers or chapters, and later read them from behind a podium, Franklin engaged and connected. He showed genuine interest in who we were and what we were doing as young scholars. His lecturing approach dismantled what Laura Rendón (2009) later discussed as the "agreement of separation" in teaching and learning that, in part, creates and maintains distance between teachers and students, and between students and subject matter.

For Franklin, history was highly personal and frequently connected to direct lived experience. He made these connections explicit in his auto-biography, *Mirror to America* (2005), and in publication of *My Life and an Era* (1997), his father's autobiography that Franklin coedited with his son. Both books are studies in intercultural relations and separations told through direct observation, participation, and two-way reflection. Both are also critical reflections on the United States that clearly show that race matters and affects the distribution of power and opportunity, even within a family that achieved remarkable results in the advancement of civil rights.

Although never abandoning the canons of historical scholarship, Franklin disclosed his own lived experiences in describing broader themes applicable to others. His life was a personal and societal "mirror to America" much as his father's life exemplified the dynamics of an era. Gently but intentionally, he connected his life with ours and expressed moral obligations to pursue equity and inclusion. These qualities have important implications for inter-actions with students, academic disciplines, and teaching in general. From Franklin, I gained an appreciation of the immediacy and intimacy of history for all of us and the capacity to skillfully interweave experience and historical thinking skills together. He also taught me the value of direct connectivity with students. I now consciously try to use that approach in my teaching by inviting students to bring all of themselves to historical interpretation by interacting directly with source materials and using their voices to explain the past rather than the voice of another historian.

***

I knew of Rendón's early published scholarship in graduate school but came to fuller appreciation of it as I entered postgraduate professional work. Her article "From the Barrio to the Academy: Revelations of a Mexican Ameri-can Scholarship Girl" (1992) was very different in tone and content from other higher education publications that I read. Her story of being a transfer student at a major research university far from home and family in Texas revealed to me the cultural separation that can occur within institutions. The choice between one's "native culture" and "academic culture" was both foreign and tragic to me. As a privileged White male with a college-educated father who insisted on my own college enrollment from earliest memory, there was no appreciable cultural difference between my academic life and family life. I had no cultural choices to make or familial consequences to suffer as a result of higher education. To learn that others did was startling. Rendón's story made me think about how academic norms and processes become tools of cultural isolation rather than inclusion. It made me wonder about students who are removed from their cultural moorings through academic expectations that often disrespect key elements of cultural identity and experience. Later, it made me think about my own teaching practices and whether my pedagogy invited students in or left them out. Rendón, like Franklin, became part of my community of practitioners that challenged me to rethink my practices and to become more intentional in pursuing intercultural pedagogy.

Sometimes I would forget past guidance that I received experientially or through scholarship. Reflecting on it, I believe that my best opportunities for developing skill with intercultural pedagogy came through interacting with skillful and reflective practitioners; soliciting and listening carefully to student voices about what does and does not work in learning environments and learning assessments; reading a broad array of scholarship on teaching, learning, and ways of knowing; and reflecting on and debriefing with others (e.g., teaching and research assistants) what did and did not work in classroom interactions. Although this is not an all-inclusive list, it is representative of the multiple factors that contribute to successful teaching and learning within multicultural spaces.

(Catherine) Three years after returning from Thailand, I enrolled in one of the top family science graduate programs. I remember that as I learned about my field of study, I was continually questioning how theories, measures, and interpretations of research findings were influenced by culture. My personal experiences told me that the meanings and expressions of couple-hood, marriage, parenting, child development, grandparenting, elder care, and other family relationships and processes were significantly culture-bound. However, I also remember feeling inadequate because I couldn't cite literature or speak in a "scholarly manner" about what I knew to be true—that culture deeply shapes experiences and meanings of family.

For example, I questioned the applicability of the family resource management framework to Thai culture. Family resource management involves decisions and behaviors by which families allocate resources, such as time and money, to achieve family goals. The framework starts with an assumption that one can control one's destiny and that the future is dependent on the intentional allocation of scarce resources to achieve goals and improve one's quality of life. These assumptions could be called into question in

Thai culture, where karma and luck significantly shape one's worldview. This questioning propelled me to conduct my master's research in Thailand, examining the applicability of the family resource management framework. I actually found that the framework could be applied to the agrarian families in my study. However, they described planning in ways that were different from Euro-American conceptions of resource management; it was more circular than linear, more present- than future-focused. Their planning horizons were much shorter and typically followed a seasonal rather than a calendar-based rhythm.

Over time, I came to recognize that my questioning and feelings of inadequacy reflected the ways the academic world (or culture) has constructed our sense of "legitimate" ways of knowing. The "producers" of knowledge are primarily scholars who are grounded in a Western scientific paradigm—either by birth or by training. We have concluded that what is considered "knowledge" or "truth" is only that which has undergone rigorous scientific testing and verification. I share a more recent example of how I am reminded of this normalized range of "acceptable" knowledge. Since 2006, I have developed a relationship with a local organization in northern Thailand that is working to preserve the Mekong River, its tributaries, and its watershed. My Thai colleagues are clear that their role is to bring the peoples' knowledge to the table when decisions are made that could impact the river and the lives of the people who depend on it. They have a healthy skepticism about research that is conducted by university professors, who typically study small segments of the river. My colleagues question their results, noting that researchers don't understand that the river is a living organism and is constantly changing. They also point out that results based on measurements of physical properties of the river alone without consideration of local peoples' knowledge and experience with the river will lead to inaccurate conclusions.

My river story illustrates a norm that research rigor is recognized only when it fits the Western scientific paradigm, leaving little room for novel ideas and alternate constructions of reality. This is also true for family research. The tension between what is considered valid based on a particular paradigm or worldview pushes against the realities of families from different cultures. Our knowledge of families continues to be centered on dominant culture realities with a nod to "variation" when other experiences differ from that norm.

***

But even community-based, culturally relevant research faces time and effort challenges. Collaborators must grapple with being culturally and linguistically sound, navigate the protocols and requirements that pertain to human subjects research, interpret data across insider-outsider perspectives, negotiate writing contributions and language facility, and honor collaborators' unique needs for publishing. The resulting scholarship can be groundbreaking, offering new knowledge and insights into families who exist in their nested social, cultural, economic, political, and religious environments. However, the barriers erected by our tenure processes prohibit significant investment in this work, work that is not expedient or scalable, at least initially. (I recall a faculty mentor saying to me early in my career, "I know your heart is in international work. But get tenure first—then you can pursue those goals.") Intensive qualitative exploratory research that is a necessary prerequisite to being able to ask appropriate research questions and develop measures that are culturally valid and reliable is generally not publishable in top-tier journals, those that are noted for their high-impact factors, again a long-held criterion to which scholars have ascribed and upheld for decades. Thus, junior faculty especially are forced to make an untenable choice between conducting research that breaks new ground and pushes the boundaries of our knowledge and staying the course, conducting studies using secondary quantitative data or methodologies that privilege participants from the dominant culture in order to publish . . . or perish. The tenure clock ticks too fast for products of community-engaged research or international scholarship to reach the stage of "counting"—that is, a published peer-reviewed article in a U.S.-based journal. Thus institutional and disciplinary norms that shape our academic lives push against our commitment to research that privileges the voices, perspectives, and experiences of those who are largely absent in our literature.

Pause for reflection and writing. We encourage you to take some time now to think and write about your beliefs about the nature of knowledge and what has influenced the development of your current teaching and scholarly pedagogy.

Invitation for Reflection

1. *What are my beliefs around how knowledge is created and who is responsible for academic knowledge?*
2. *Who or what had the most influence on my understanding of "what" I am teaching?*

Self as Teacher and Scholar

(Bob) Over the last 25 years, subsequent to my doctoral training, I read works by Laura Rendón, Sylvia Hurtado, and Jonathan Kozol. Much more recently I've read works by bell hooks, Paulo Freire, Vine Deloria, Daniel Wildcat,

Michael Apple, Parker Palmer, and many others. In a sense, this collection of scholars created tension with my discipline of history. These authors thought about and responded to the kinds of learning relationships and transactions that occur between students and teachers, between students and students, and also about the politics and power dynamics of knowledge and knowing (Apple 1982, 1990; Deloria & Wildcat, 2001). This stood in contrast to what disciplinary content was covered and delivered *to* students. From the lens of my training as a historian, I was concerned about whether I taught the Civil War well by covering the complex social, military, technological, and political dynamics of that conflict. Conversely, scholars of intercultural pedagogy urged me to think about how I taught that information and whether students and their diverse perspectives were part of the historical investigation.

Nonhistorians made me think more critically about how I taught as a historian and more deeply about how I interacted with students rather than solely what I delivered to students. When I began teaching U.S. history, I did all the work, all the talking, all the interpreting. My course evaluations were fine—probably because students knew I loved being there, cared about them (despite my teaching approach), and really enjoyed the subject matter. But I was soon troubled by thoughts of what students were actually retaining as they left my content-laden lecture-based course and went onward with their lives. There was little to no course connection with or relevance to their lives; there was far too little inclusion of voices from multiple cultures and ethnicities who lived within the vast expanse of the United States and the ways they made sense of their existence. Also, I did not learn early enough what students were curious about and how they learned best.

I began thinking about what I heard from students in review sessions and their test responses. Overwhelmingly, I heard my voice, not theirs. In review sessions much the same happened—my voice being articulated by students rather than their own thoughts and interpretations. By far, the most repeated question in review sessions was, "Can I say . . .?" as students sought permission and approval from me—the authority—for what they might write in their exam responses.

A few years ago, based upon student feedback that they enjoyed visuals, I replaced many text-heavy PowerPoint slides with photographs of New York City streets teeming with wagons, horses, people of every variety, and tenement housing with clothing lines strung from window to window. I added discussion questions that would surely engage diverse students in insightful multicultural conversation around historical topics. A sure bet, I thought, would be a class session on immigration to American cities in the late nineteenth and early twentieth centuries.

In class, I went through each photo slowly, let the students soak in the full force of the images, and then expectantly turned it over to small groups guided by my discussion questions. The initial promising sound of voices died out within three minutes, and the full-group discussion was disengaged, surface-level in the power of observation, and disheartening in the quality of historical interpretation. Clearly, something had gone wrong despite my efforts.

Gradually, I realized that I missed something else that students told me was important to them—relevance or personal connection to the content. This was a foundational tension in the course. I had a multicultural class of students and multicultural historical content but no connections or interactions between the two. My pedagogy failed to make the connections, and my discussion questions were still self-generated and served to exclude the perspectives and lived experiences of my students. Clearly, multicultural content, multicultural students, and visuals of multicultural communities did not equate with intercultural pedagogy and communication; the dynamics of intercultural conversation, teaching, and learning were missing.

As intercultural competency scholars Gesche and Makeham (2008) observe,

> Students are not likely to gain intercultural competenc[e] by osmosis alone; they must be exposed in practices and understandings of the "other" and actively involved in an intercultural experience. That can be achieved through purposeful tasks through which they can develop the capacity to observe, to explore, to listen and to ask questions. (p. 247)

It took time to reflect, experiment, and revise pedagogical approaches and my own notions of history as a discipline and students as participants in historical meaning-making. It took time to trust students as historical questioners, investigators, and interpreters in their own right and to provide the means for them to interact and learn from one another. I needed to move from being simply a master of content to also being a non-master of intercultural pedagogy—a tension that is always present but well worth having. Sometimes I felt like I was breaching the intellectual standards of my discipline. For example, could student experience and expectations of relevance be honored and utilized in rigorous historical investigation and interpretation without succumbing to "presentism," trivializing the past, or establishing false connections between dissimilar peoples and times? It took time to think carefully about these questions and my responses to them. I conferred with colleagues, listened to students, and read unfamiliar genres of scholarship. I pulled from the social sciences as well as the humanities. I even borrowed from the physical sciences to discover different ways to engage diverse students in intellectual problem-solving (Lattery, 2009). I needed to bridge different forms of intellectual inquiry and the disciplinary cultural differences and dissonances between them. Again, it necessitated substantial personal development through new learning and experimentation.

(Catherine) Barriers to developing intercultural pedagogy and globalized teaching and learning exist in the academy. The tension between investing time to conduct research, publish, and secure external funding and investing time in developing one's teaching portfolio and pedagogy is particularly intense in the tenure process. Good teaching is valued; in my department, one cannot achieve tenure and promotion without evidence of quality teaching. However, investment in teaching improvement is fairly rare. If faculty members haven't been trained in intercultural pedagogy in their graduate programs, it probably isn't going to develop once they start their academic careers. And my sense is that graduate training in disciplines like mine rarely includes much about teaching pedagogy at all, let alone intercultural pedagogy or infusing global perspectives in courses.

In the void left by a lack of attention to training teachers, I also speculate that my cohorts' research training as positivists or postpositivists to become experts, to create new knowledge, to search for the truth by using appropriate theory and rigorous methodology, was applied in the classroom. It was assumed that if you knew "the content," you could teach it. Thus teachers focused on content and students absorbed their knowledge; learning spaces became extensions of the research lab. Coconstructing knowledge and questioning racial and cultural biases in our knowledge base involved too much time and were considered to be too process-focused at the expense of content.

Like so many others, I have primarily developed my intercultural pedagogy through my personal experiences—not in the academy. Although I believe my instincts are generally good and I trust that my personal experiences have been fairly effective in informing my teaching, I am a good example of what we wrote in chapter 1: *Without a guiding framework, one is left to ad hoc "good intentions," a piecemeal approach. One is also left without a community of theorist-practitioners with whom to dialogue and challenge ourselves* (p. 4).

***

In 2006 I was assigned to teach a course titled Global and Diverse Families. I inherited an approved syllabus that was approved to meet a core liberal education requirement. It needed to address globalization, diversity, and critical thinking as well as have a research skills development component. I taught the course as written, focusing on families in various cultural groups each week. I adopted a typical family discipline text that used a comparative approach to help learners know "about" families (marriage, aging, child-rearing, etc.) from various regions of the world.

It wasn't long into the semester that I became discontent with the syllabus and the way I was teaching; it didn't fit with the way I understand families and culture. The course design was fine for considering cultural generalities, but was that enough? Students in our major would be working with families in a variety of family-serving community organizations. With the knowledge they gained in my course, would they assume a person or family from a particular culture fit the generalized patterns they'd learned? Did they comprehend the variation within cultures as well as across cultures? Was comparing generalities about culture creating rigid categories in which they'd place people and block them from considering whether they fit, or how life experiences or other social location characteristics such as race, education, class, gender, religion, or migration experience had influenced them? They struggled to consider the influences of economics, politics, religion, climate, or history on customs and practices in a particular culture.

When the waves of refugees arrived in Minnesota beginning in the late 1970s, we weren't ready for it. Fast-forward to the twenty-first century when the children of those immigrant and refugee families are in our classrooms; for me, this is a very exciting change from the homogenous student body that characterized my own undergraduate experience. As I reflected on the increasing cultural diversity of our learners and the increasing cultural diversity of the families with whom they will work after graduation, my discomfort with how I was teaching my course grew and I was compelled to consider how I might change the way I taught it. Our graduates need to understand the transnational nature of families in today's global reality. This goes beyond considering extended family locally to embrace that families enact relationships and share resources across great geographical distances. They need to know how to interact with people in ways that respect values, beliefs, behaviors, and traditions that may be different than their own. They need to recognize that their assumptions about experiencing family are based in their own cultural socialization. They need some cultural generalized knowledge about families from a variety of cultures, but they need to hold that knowledge as a starting place for developing a relationship and learning more. Cranton (2001) encourages teachers to be more authentic in integrating the "self" and the "teacher." For me, this meant that my own journey of learning about myself as a cultural being could inform how I help learners with that same process.

Pause for reflection and writing. We encourage you to take some time now to think and write about your development as teacher and scholar.

Invitation for Reflection

1. *What is a critical learning moment that shaped how I see myself as teacher?*
2. *How do I use my experiences, skills, knowledge, and awareness to support my students' intercultural development?*

PART TWO

FROM THEORY TO ACTION

We began this book with the observation that "a profound shift is necessary in the daily, local practices of teaching and learning in order to more fully utilize and honor human difference in higher education and to maximize learning in our classrooms" (p. 3). Our own pedagogical journeys underscore and are propelled by this reality. While colleges and universities continue to struggle with issues involving access, equity, retention, campus climate, and other important elements of social justice, we do have within our classrooms highly diverse student populations that can deeply enrich teaching and learning. To do so, we must commit to substantively and skillfully engaging students in ways that invite, encourage, and use their diversity as a central part of teaching and learning. This requires ongoing critical assessment of our practices and continued restless revision of intercultural pedagogy.

In chapters 1 and 2, we advocated for three agreements, or core values, that characterize intercultural pedagogy. In chapter 3 you considered others' and your own process of coming to more complex intercultural awareness and of developing intercultural pedagogy. But how do we habituate ourselves to actualizing those values? It is likely that we have adopted habitual practices after observing and experiencing teaching over many years as students. From designing a course to facilitating the classroom environment, to engaging students and assessing outcomes, we need to ensure that our habits of action reflect and support our agreements or values. Does our syllabus prioritize activities that are congruent with our goals? Do our use of class time and our direction to students about their out-of-class time reflect the values and our goals? Or are they in conflict? Are we assessing the learning outcomes we most value? Are we soliciting evidence of those outcomes in forms that best invite and reflect students' development? Without this conscious critique of our habits of action, we are not able to make decisions or establish intentional habits of intercultural pedagogy.

As we have stated before, real teaching happens in complex, "live," or dynamic environments that involve real (and thus complex and dynamic) people who have different experiences and perspectives. A viable pedagogical framework will be one that provides a scaffold of key values of an intercultural approach; it must not merely be prescriptive or dogmatic, but be responsive to the interplay of theory/practice, concepts/contexts. In our collective experience, however, scholarship often tends to emphasize theory *or* practice, and it can be difficult to find rich exemplars of this dialectic nature of pedagogical work—the ongoing interplay between theory, practice, and reflection wherein activity in one prompts activity in another and, ultimately, change. When examples are provided, they are often supplemental to the rich theoretical framework of a given book or chapter or article.

In chapters 4 and 5, we address this gap, putting forward and exploring from our own work in its imperfect and still evolving forms. Bob and Catherine bring us into different phases of their course design, instruction, assessment, and interactions with and among students, charting their process of developing intercultural pedagogy in their respective courses. Bob focuses on a general education, undergraduate U.S. history course. Catherine focuses on a required introductory course within her undergraduate major in family social science. We chose these two courses because they provide both specific and distinct examples of the developmental process, while they also illustrate what we believe are familiar demands and pressures instructors encounter (from institutions, programs, and students) as they are seeking to transform received courses and courses that fulfill a particular niche.

We also offer these two case studies because they help to make visible, or to bring us inside of, the process of transforming a course. For many of us, the idea of *transforming* our courses and the way we teach seems overwhelming, even impossible. Some might frame the choice as transform or do nothing, become an intercultural expert or ignore intercultural development completely, focus on your disciplinary content or focus on "skills." We would like to challenge this; binary thinking affirms stasis and rewards the idea that if one simply doesn't have *enough* (enough time, enough expertise, enough incentive, enough support), it is best to do nothing. It is often assumed that the more we teach the "better" we get. We would also suggest that one can approach the development/integration of intercultural pedagogy as a series of actions and as a shift in awareness and intention that is incorporated over time into our student interactions, syllabi, learning activities, and assessment. Throughout this book, you will find reflection questions, activities, and prompts to support your own development of intercultural pedagogy within the particular context in which you are operating. We invite you to engage alongside us with your course in mind (and in hand) to consider alternatives and changes conducive to "interculturalizing" your pedagogy and course design.

4

CASE STUDY

Bob

> If we truly wish our students to understand the past, it is not enough to ask them to simply consume our expert knowledge. Rather, we must invite them into our realm—the realm of historical discourse—and encourage them to construct historical knowledge for themselves. (Sipress & Voelker, 2009, p. 33)

A few years ago, I discovered practices and tensions in my teaching that surprised me. One involved how I thought about and lived within my disciplinary field of history. Outside of my classroom I was energized by the discovery of primary sources and the ability to create interpretative historical meaning from archival materials, but inside the classroom I felt the energy-draining repetition of large sums of course content and lecturing. Wanting to reconcile those differences, I began exploring ways to have my students experience the excitement of historical discovery and interpretation, while liberating them—and myself—from too much content delivered only by me.

Another discovery, intertwined with the first, focused on the value of diversity and intercultural interactions within my classroom. Although I sincerely professed my passion for diverse lived experience and intercultural communication with students, my work as a teacher did little to use or honor student experience and interaction. Inspired by historians such as Ronald Takaki and the very best teachers I had as a student, I resolved to better integrate diverse voices as a means of exploring the past, including those voices present in my own classroom. It takes humility and trust to not dominate all instructional space and to acknowledge that students have something of value to offer to disciplinary study through dialogue and direct interaction with historical sources (Freire, 1970).

These discoveries did not come as sudden epiphanies. Rather, they emerged over time as growing tensions or dissonances. In reflecting on them,

I see the persistent grip of conventional beliefs and practices within disciplines and teaching. I taught mostly as I was taught within my discipline—through content-heavy lectures. I was also captive to my own limiting notions of the discipline and how I should teach. Over time, through combinations of many small changes and some larger course and pedagogical overhauls, I was able to resolve the biggest tensions in how I lived as a historian and as a teacher. With intention, I moved to eliminate the dichotomy of professing the value of diversity and intercultural interaction within my classrooms while enacting practices that unintentionally did the reverse.

This chapter describes much of my journey in weaving together my discipline with intercultural pedagogy, a powerful and yet not obvious process of intertwining. For me, it required reaching beyond disciplinary literature and practices to scholars of multicultural teaching and learning (e.g., Calder, Cutler, & Mills Kelly, 2002; Merriam & Assoc., 2007; Rendón, 2009). The journey has links to many of the themes that we include in other chapters and particularly to the values of intercultural pedagogy that we describe in chapter 2. Deeply imbedded in the pedagogical decisions and actions described here are the values of pursuing equity and inclusion in classrooms, of recognizing that expertise is fluid and developmental, and of engaging in ongoing pedagogical reflection and revision.

These values were pursued simultaneously, and the process was not linear. While I was intentionally pursuing equity and inclusion within my classroom, I was also reflecting on how I might revise specific parts of my pedagogy to further build equity and inclusion into the course. In keeping with the sentiment that expertise is fluid and developmental, no final destination is described here. It is a continuous journey of discovering, experimenting, assessing, tweaking, sometimes completely overhauling, and improving. However, documented here are important changes that gave me new coherence as a disciplinary practitioner of intercultural pedagogy. Best of all, the journey to this point has also provided new vitality and purpose in what I share through engaging history with my students.

Reconnecting With the Fundamentals of My Discipline

I enjoy being a historian. There is a real thrill in working with original artifacts of the past that tell important stories with diverse voices. Within archival collections I regularly discover largely unpublished histories of civil rights activism that are contained in letters, cards, notebooks, photos, telegrams, and institutional documents. In one large archival collection, I recently found a file folder containing Thurgood Marshall's law school report card from the early 1930s. This fascinating document, annotated with brief handwritten comments by his professors, foreshadowed Marshall's future greatness as a lawyer and U.S. Supreme Court justice. In another collection I came across the tattered courtroom transcription of a 1933 murder trial in a rural Virginia community where a Black defendant was accused of killing two White women. The skill of an all–African American legal defense team miraculously saved the defendant from the death penalty and further legitimized the work of Black lawyers in the Jim Crow South (part of this case will soon be used with students in a classroom activity or history problem).

I want to bring the same joy of intellectual discovery and use of interpretive voice into my 1000-level U.S. history course. I want my students to engage the discipline as historians and, in the process, engage one another as a community of historians who have different perspectives rooted in differing lived experiences. I want to create the personal connections and disciplinary skills that spark the kind of energy and interest that first drew me into a love for history.

Revisiting what my discipline is and what historians purport to do proved an important starting point in building a revised course that provides students with a realistic experience of being a historian. Gurung, Chick, and Haynie (2009) refer to this process as identifying "signature pedagogies" that unite the discipline with teaching practices. In their words, "signature pedagogies invoke the core characteristics of a discipline to help students think like a biologist, a creative writer, or a sociologist, rather than simply expecting them to passively accept the analysis or findings of an expert who already thinks like a biologist, a creative writer, or a sociologist" (p. 4).

Consistent with this observation, I needed to move the methods from my own work with historical sources into the classroom for students to experience themselves. The skills and methods I use as a historian shifted over time from the explicit, conscious actions of a novice to the intuitive and subconscious movements of a more experienced practitioner. I needed to re-explore the "core characteristics" of my discipline in order to bring them into the classroom pedagogically.

To reconnect with explicit explanations of what historians do, I reread numerous books written by historians about history as a discipline and as a profession (Barzun & Graff, 1977; Bloch, 1953; Carr, 1961; Commager, 1965; Elton, 1967; Fischer, 1970; Handlin, 1979; Nevins, 1963; Stern, 1973; Tuchman, 1981), many of which I had first encountered in graduate school. After exhausting those books, I pursued newer sources I had not yet read, searching for points of intersection on what it is historians do and perhaps how they do it (Andrews & Burke, 2007; Ayers, 2005; Calder, 2006; Evans, 1999; Lerner, 1997; Marius & Page, 2005; Rampolla, 2015; Sipress & Voelker, 2009; Wood, 2008).

Although challenging because historians sometimes disagree with one another about what history is as a field as well as the nature of their work, the investigation was rewarding. It helped me to focus on essential skills for historical thinking that undergraduate students can grasp, use, and remember. The main theme culled from all of these sources was *history framed as problem-solving*. Marius and Page (2005) observed, "historians are curious and relentless questioners. . . . Historians find a puzzle and try to solve it" (p. 2). To approach historical problems effectively entails identifying requisite historical thinking skills, so I sought to identify the historical thinking skills necessary to address historical problems and to enable students to engage sources and one another within disciplinary norms.

Andrews and Burke (2007) compress the elements of historical thinking into five "Cs": *change over time, causality, context, complexity,* and *contingency*. This short list of thinking skills is of great utility given that it encompasses much of what historians investigate and think about. The brevity of the list enables me to use it substantively with my students within a single semester. Pedagogically, it necessitates moving away from a lecture-only format to one of demonstration, active discussion, experimentation, review, repetition, and active engagement with peers and source materials. It requires that students use their minds and voices without answers being given to them. I see this as a deliberate pathway to intercultural communication, sharing, and learning.

In the first few weeks of class, students gain experience in how historians establish the context—one of the five Cs—for a period, person, or event that is being studied. Context-setting involves thinking about a variety of pertinent elements that have importance for the way in which what is being studied is situated in time. It may involve highly complex combinations of geography, demography, politics, societal beliefs, actions of government, socially constructed meanings of race and gender, the history that immediately precedes what is studied, and so forth.

To make this more manageable, historians ask questions to focus or narrow that which is pertinent to context (as well as the other "Cs" of historical thinking). An example of this comes from my freshman-level history course, where we use Frederick Douglass's speech, "What the Black Man Wants," early in the semester. Douglass delivered the speech in April 1865, which was an important transitional moment in the history of the United States. Using the Douglass speech, students consider the following questions in my class and then construct written responses:

- What is the context of the time in which Douglass delivers this speech? Investigate and describe what is happening in the United States in April 1865 in relation to Douglass's speech.
- What does Douglass indicate that the Black man wants? (Hint: He wants multiple things—not just the most direct response to this question!)

- Why does he want it? (Be as thorough as possible—again, there are multiple reasons why.)
- What will the Black man be if he receives what he wants? (This involves you doing historical interpretation.)
- What, according to Douglass, will be lost if the Black man is denied what he wants? (Again, be as thorough as possible.)
- What other questions should we as historians ask about this document?

Many of these questions are contextual in nature. The questions require students to engage the reading rather than being told about the speech and the time in which it was delivered. Students are also expected to ask their own questions as historians to further the conversation around this source within their small discussion groups and later with the full class.

As students research and explore what was occurring in April 1865, they use contemporary research tools that are readily available and sometimes frowned upon in classrooms—cell phones, iPads, and laptops. Learners can quickly access contextual information from a variety of sources using wireless devices, gathering the information and then sharing their findings within small teams. Although this does require significant allocations of classroom time (and expectations regarding how they will use the devices and stay on task), it is well worth it given what students discover and share as active historians in collaboration with peers. By actively searching for contexts surrounding the speech, students begin uncovering and appreciating the nuances, opportunities, and urgencies that Douglass worked within as he composed and delivered "What the Black Man Wants."

In the following section I describe how, over several semesters, I carefully winnowed out much content "coverage" of particular periods of U.S. history delivered only by my voice. Moving from content-centric lecturing to more active student participation made room for skill development in historical thinking and contributed to the goals of fostering active learning and more substantive intercultural communication between members of the class. Freeing myself from the "the tyranny of content" opened these spaces and supported increased equity and inclusion in the learning space.

Invitation for Reflection

1. *What are the core characteristics of my discipline? How do I—or how can I—bring those characteristics into my classroom for students to experience?*
2. *How do the core characteristics of my discipline invite engagement? How can students interact with me and with one another through disciplinary inquiry?*

From "Content Coverage" to Intercultural Discovery and Discussion: Redesigning a Pedagogical Approach

> Narration (with the teacher as narrator) leads the students to memorize mechanically the narrated content. Worse yet, it turns them into "containers," into "receptacles" to be "filled" by the teacher. (Freire, 1970, pp. 52–53)

Historians love content. We are trained in undergraduate and graduate programs to master and respect content through lectures given by experts in the field, research assignments, and examination processes. Later, in our professional academic lives, we contribute to content through publication of articles and books. We take great pleasure in reading multiple interpretations of moments and eras in time to see how different historians approach the complexities of topics. A casual look at my own shelves reveals more than seven dozen studies relating to the U.S. Civil War (this is not hyperbole—it is all too real). Near those volumes are more than 150 books on the civil rights movements of the 1930s–1960s (with 8 just on the NAACP). Each volume has a different interpretation—the historian who wrote it has a voice and perspective that differ from another historian writing within the same topical area. I love content as much as any other disciplinary colleague. It informs my work and enables me to experience the complexities of the past.

On its own, I do not see this as a negative. Yet in the case of my teaching, too much content led to rote memorization (reinforced by assessment designs that depended on and rewarded memorization); the dominance of my interpretative voice; an absence of original voice from students; a lack of multicultural interaction within the classroom (there was little time for it given all that needed "covering"); and a feeling that history is a detached discipline vacant of any personal meaning. As Freire (1970) noted, it worked to dishonor and disengage students by denying them opportunity to participate in and contribute to knowledge production. I made the decision to change that reality. Change required letting go of a good portion of course content that was precious to me and making space for student engagement and discipline-based skill development (Calder, 2006).

Editing Course Content to Make Room for Intercultural Pedagogy

To begin the process of content reduction, I used a summer break to reprint and review the course syllabus and all of my PowerPoints. It was a hefty pile. The PowerPoints alone ran well over 200 pages, with three slides on each page (meaning, yes, I was using more than 600 slides in 30 class sessions over 15 weeks).

The PowerPoints told a clear story. The following sample (Figure 4.1) from 2011 demonstrates in part the content-heavy question and answer format that I used. Pedagogically, I posed and answered *all* of the questions for *every* class session. Students knew that the questions at the top of each set of PowerPoints were potential essay exam questions and, as a result, they paid particularly close attention to my responses to the questions. "Mindless" rote memorization tended to occur and, as you will see, exam responses were

Figure 4.1. Harlem Renaissance questions.

Example from 2011

The "Harlem Renaissance" Questions

- What is a renaissance?

- What is the significance of the Harlem Renaissance?

- What did this renaissance produce and communicate? In what ways did the products of the Harlem Renaissance reflect the meaning of "renaissance"?

Students all knew that these were potential exam questions so they were careful to listen only to my interpretations in order to get the "right" answer.
This was mostly a lecture-based format with me as the authority on the subject matter.

Here I form all of the questions and immediately answer them in the slide that follows this one. This left very little to no room for students to engage each other or to develop interpretive voice and skills.

Example from 2011

The "Harlem Renaissance"

- Takes place at the end of WWI (1919) through the mid-1930s

- **Renaissance** = "Rebirth," "born again," "enthusiastic and rigorous activity along literary, artistic, and cultural lines distinguished by a revival of interest in the past, by an increasing pursuit of learning, and by an imaginative response to broader horizons generally" (*Webster's New International English Dictionary*)

- Was burst of African American expression in literature, essays, painting, music, plays, etc.— exploring Black consciousness, experience, and power of self-expression and definition.

Here I answer all of the questions posed in the prior slide. This made me appear as the only authority on the subject matter and provided narrow answers for students to memorize rather than inviting their own interpretations.

essentially my voice being repeated rather than those of the students as individual interpretive historians (Langer, 1997). Further, this mode of teaching discouraged multicultural student interaction given that the course, the materials, and the assessments were all focused on my interpretations and, therefore, there really was no need or incentive to hear from or to interact with anyone else.

The absence of student interaction and meaning-making in classrooms is often documented in course assessments. This was certainly so in my course as students submitted exam responses. In these two examples from student exams (Figures 4.2 and 4.3), it is easy to identify how students were simply repeating the PowerPoint text I provided. Most of the exam responses were

Figure 4.2. Harlem Renaissance exam response: Student 1.

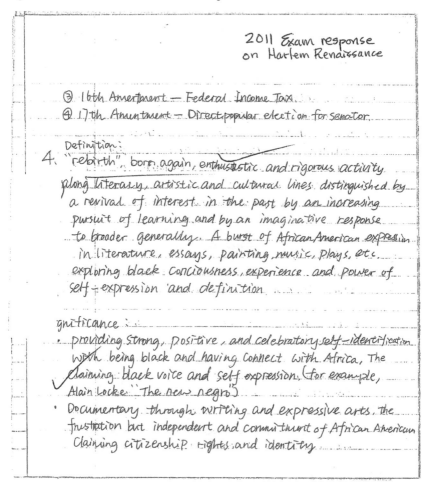

very similar in content and phrasing. My process of lecturing and using Power-Points to underscore key questions and answers provided no room for students to personally discover and explore the meaning of a renaissance or the expression of a renaissance in primary source materials, such as visual art, essays, poems, letters, music, and other forms of expression.

To change this reality, I modified my pedagogical approach. I had to make difficult decisions regarding where to cut or heavily edit content. A central part of the process was removing much of my voice and replacing it with room for student voices and interpretations to emerge within the classroom.

Figure 4.3. Harlem Renaissance exam response: Student 2.

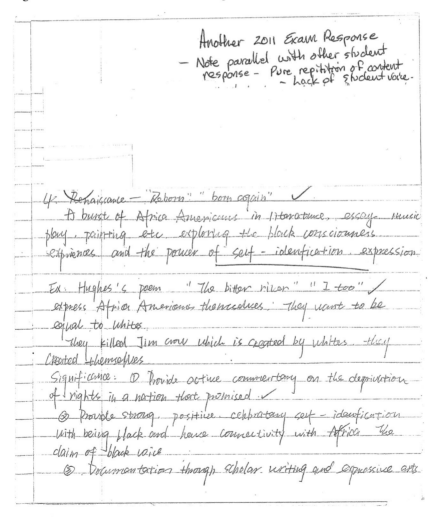

As documented here, the PowerPoints from 2015 represent a significant shift from content delivery to historical thinking skill development so that students can bring their own informed voices to interpreting the past. Rather than providing full responses to problem-related questions, students were given historical information/data related to the questions so that they might express their own interpretations in consultation with one another. To begin, I removed my answers to questions from the PowerPoints so that singular responses from me were no longer the norm. As PowerPoint slides were subtracted, room for student discovery was added. In place of providing my answers, students researched important terms and concepts. They did this in small teams rather than as solitary historians. Cell phones, laptops, and iPads stayed on tabletops as research tools. Searching for the meaning of *renaissance* did not take much time. Students were free to pursue the meaning on any site and they discovered definitions that, although consistent, differed from one another in phrasing and enhanced understanding of the word.

With definitions in hand, we eased further into contextualizing the Harlem Renaissance and how the poetry, essays, novels, performing arts, and fashion of that place and time signaled "rebirth" and transition for

Figure 4.4. Harlem Renaissance artists.

2015 Examples

Harlem Renaissance Artists & the "New Negro"

Primary Sources:

- Paintings of Aaron Douglas and Alan Freelon
- Sculpture of Augusta Savage
- Writing of W. A. Domingo: The New Negro—What Is He? (1920)

Secondary Source

- Peter N. Nelson, *A More Unbending Battle: The Harlem Hellfighters' Struggle for Freedom in WWI and Equality at Home* (2009), pp. 260–261.

Figure 4.5. Harlem Renaissance—The "New Negro."

"The New Negro . . . didn't feel like pretending, did not agree to live in a separate, parallel society. He did not want to work slowly, was neither patient nor accommodating, and believed that God wanted the same thing he wanted—a society where African Americans lived freely and safely as equals, with dignity and self-respect. Such ideas existed before the war, in moderation and in the extreme, just as the old ideas persisted after the war. The difference was that the war provided black Americans with a new role model, the modern colored soldier hero."

Source. Peter N. Nelson, *A More Unbending Battle: The Harlem Hellfighters' Struggle for Freedom in WWI and Equality at Home* (2009), pp. 260–261.

Figure 4.6. Aaron Douglas, *Aspects of Negro Life: From Slavery to Reconstruction.*

Harlem Renaissance: Aaron Douglas

Note. From The New York Public Library (https://digitalcollections.nypl.org/items/634ad849-7832-309e-e040-e00a180639bb)

African Americans. Students interpreted the notions of "the New Negro," or rebirth or being born again, in African American paintings and sculpture (Figure 4.4). We jointly discovered written historical interpretations, such as that of Peter Nelson, and the paintings of Aaron Douglas (Figures 4.5 and 4.6). My voice and words were gradually reduced, and student interactions and voices increased in each class session.

This shift facilitated much more multicultural interaction than ever before and also enabled students to express historical meaning in their own voices and use all of their cultural identity and experiences in the process. I was no longer the source or filter for such interpretations but, rather, more a facilitator of historical thinking skill development. Mostly gone is the rote memorization and recitation of my interpretations. In their place is the capacity for each student to be an interpretive historian who engages the discipline in a manner that replicates what historians actually do in collaboration with diverse colleagues.

As the 2011 and 2015 PowerPoint examples included here show, it took several years to reduce the course content, highlight student voices, and focus on skill development. Motivated by increasing positive results (measured in large part by the quality of student interactions and the sophistication of small group and collective responses to difficult questions), I continued removing or reframing other content. Rather than students being empty containers into which factual information is poured and then emptied in exam responses (Freire, 1970), students are now recognized and trusted as being capable of generating intercultural disciplinary knowledge. Space that was previously precluded by my race to get through World War II and into the Cold War period is provided through content reduction to develop disciplinary thinking skills and to have informed student inquiry emerge.

Invitation for Reflection

1. *How can I make room within my course for student voices to emerge? Does my course include too much content and too little space for student engagement?*
2. *How can the dominance of my voice be reduced and the emergence of multicultural student voices and interpretations be enhanced?*
3. *How can the revision of my course materials create more opportunities for students to interact with each other and to develop their disciplinary skills?*
4. *Do I believe that students are capable of generating intercultural disciplinary knowledge? If so, how do I invite and facilitate the emergence of such knowledge?*

Bringing the Work of Historians Into the Classroom: From Textbooks and Exams to "History Problems"

> The teaching of history, more than any other discipline, is dominated by textbooks. And students are right: the books are boring. The stories that history textbooks tell are predictable; every problem has already been solved or is about to be solved. Textbooks exclude conflict or real suspense. (Loewen, 1995, p. 13)

The success of early engagements with content reduction and intercultural pedagogy encouraged me to continue experimenting with how to interject more opportunities for student interaction with my discipline. In particular, I wanted to pursue additional, more in-depth historical problems with my students. The purpose for doing so was to provide students with a deeper understanding of the skills that are involved in historical inquiry and also to encourage collaborative interaction so that diverse experiences, perspectives, and ways of knowing could be made a deliberate part of the course experience.

Clearing Additional Obstacles to Make Way for Problem-Based Intercultural Pedagogy: Textbooks and Tests

Recently, with the help of two insightful undergraduate teaching assistants, I realized that my course textbook was working against me. Although I argued in class that history is not neat or episodic, the textbook divided U.S. history since the Civil War into neat, episodic chunks of time. Although I professed that history was about formulating challenging questions in order to wrestle with the complexity of sources, the textbook more often than not provided explanations rather than questions. The class became increasingly aware of the need to access sources that enabled us to hear from a broad variety of persons who lived during different moments in time and realized that the textbook frequently skipped over the voices of the unelected, disenfranchised, and the un-famous.

For several years I used one of the better survey textbooks but still found these unfortunate attributes present. To partially compensate for what the text did not include—active questioning—I developed a list of questions for each chapter in the text. The textbook became a tertiary source, one so far removed from the real voices of the past and so heavily edited that it became nearly useless as a tool to develop historical thinking skills and as a multicultural source of the past.

For these reasons I decided to quit using a survey textbook in my course. At first it felt like a trapeze artist performing without a net. One immediate reality was that without a textbook I needed to provide much of the contextual information for the class. My teaching assistants assured me that I was already doing this in what remained of the PowerPoints. Also, providing the context allowed me to model how to establish context—one of the five Cs of historical thinking. I soon discovered that I was freed from additional content bondage and that I could more easily reorient the class toward more selective topics and issues that better revealed the nature of history and that developed historical thinking skills in a more effective and collaborative way. History could more readily be presented as a complex, problem-based discipline, not one so neatly packaged as to be intellectually dead.

It is also an uncomfortable fact that many U.S. history survey textbooks do not represent the voices, experiences, values, and epistemologies of the many diverse peoples of this nation. Takaki (1993) reminds us,

> While the study of the past can provide collective self-knowledge, it often reflects the scholar's particular perspective or view of the world. What happens when historians leave out many of America's peoples? What happens, to borrow the words of Adrienne Rich [1986], "when someone with the authority of a teacher" describes our society, and "you are not in it" [p. 199].

Such an experience can be disorienting—a moment of psychic disequilib-
rium, as if you looked into a mirror and saw nothing. (p. 16)

Having greater space and freedom to select texts outside of a textbook provides opportunities to use texts written by authors who better reflect the
diversity of my students. The authors speak for themselves without me para-
phrasing or truncating their thoughts. As students express interest in lived
experience within Jim Crow systems of oppression, I bring in portions of
Ralph Ellison's (1952) novel *Invisible Man*, W. E. B. Dubois's (1903/1994)
The Souls of Black Folk, and John Hope Franklin's (2005) memoir, *Mirror
to America*. When researching the ways in which assimilation attempts by
White missionaries and others affected Native American families and children, we read accounts by Luther Standing Bear, Zitkala-Sa, and other indigenous people who experienced such attempts in boarding schools. This is
repeated for different topics and problems. Increasingly, we let multicultural
historical people speak for themselves.

A wonderful by-product of this approach is providing multiple opportunities for students to experience the very different ways in which people of
different cultures experienced, perceived, and expressed their lives in different
times and places in our history. It opens the capacity to hear non-Western
voices and stories that are part of our national experience. As we noted in chapter 2, Laura Rendón (2009) speaks to the importance of this when warning
about certain "agreements" that we stumble into when teaching that inhibit
diverse voices being heard and respected. One of those agreements is "the
agreement of monoculturalism" (Rendón, 2009, p. 41), which discounts the
contributions that women, indigenous people, and ethnic/racial minorities
have made in history, art, math, science, philosophy, and literature. Within
this particular agreement, Rendón (2009) includes the following: "the almost
exclusive validation of Western structures of knowledge . . . the subjugation
of knowledge created by indigenous people and people of color" and "course
offerings that preserve the superiority of Western civilization" (p. 41).

When teaching a course on the multicultural past of what is now the
United States, it is important to break the agreement of monoculturalism
and the opposition to differing ways of knowing and attaining knowledge.
Although disciplines have some "signature" norms for investigating and
thinking about knowledge, there is still room within them for respectful
inclusion of experience and other ways of knowing and expressing knowledge. In part, having the flexibility to reach into the vast literature and spo-
ken words of diverse people reinforces to students the legitimacy and value
of those voices and, by extension, of their own.

In moving away from a fact-based textbook, I also needed to revise
the manner in which I assess student learning and knowledge. Student

assessment is an important but sometimes forgotten part of intercultural pedagogy. It can reinforce or negate our best efforts to engage multicultural students in our disciplines. It is inconsistent for me to profess that history is more vibrant and interesting than a set of facts, but test and grade for factual knowledge. If I claim that student voice is a critical component for interpretative skill building but my assessments do not allow room for student voice to be present, I have a serious pedagogical misalignment with which to contend. I experienced each of these inconsistencies with my assessments, and I had to make many adjustments to tighten the alignment between what I said was important and how I actually formed and assessed student assignments.

In 2009, I was using multiple-choice questions and short-answer essays. In re-examining them, I notice that they closely followed the fact-based information of the textbook. It is clear from many of those questions that I was checking to see if students were reading the textbook and absorbing the facts. There were no interpretive elements present in the questions or any problem-based components that would require historical thinking skills. I soon moved away from multiple-choice questions, even though my course enrollments were fairly large. I moved toward more essay questions instead, but I found that my essay questions were not much better than the multiple choice questions. Consider some the following questions or prompts that I asked on an exam in 2011:

> What are the different forms of assimilation? What was the intended outcome of assimilation? What was the impact of these assimilation attempts on Native Americans?

> Identify and describe three motivations for American imperialism.

> What were the criticisms toward American imperialism (describe at least three)?

These questions were essentially asking for what Langer (1997) refers to as "mindless" rote memorization. Historical work is not memorization—it is, as we have noted, problem-solving led by active questioning and skilled interaction with historical sources. This mode of teaching and assessment did not fit with genuine historical inquiry. Students paid attention to what I said in class or in my handouts only to discover the correct answers for tests. They paid little to no attention to what their peers said given that those responses or observations would not be on the test, thereby nullifying their legitimacy and importance in the eyes of students.

As with other adjustments I made over time, I decided to revise the course again—this time moving away from tests and PowerPoint-infused "answers" to the creation of "history problems" that required student interpretation of original sources, interaction with other students, and utilization of their own voices. I wanted their voices to "count" in learning and in assessments of learning.

Invitation for Reflection

1. *How can I bring multicultural voices and perspectives into my course content in substantive ways?*
2. *How can I make my course assessments more consistent with my pedagogy, my discipline, and with multicultural perspectives?*

Introducing and Experimenting With "History Problems"

By nature, I am a restless teacher. I want to bring into my classrooms attributes of the very best teachers that I had as an undergraduate and graduate student. In that spirit, after another summer break when I had time to construct some fuller-length "problems" and relevant sources, I began using history problems in class during the 2012–2013 academic year. The problems were intended to more fully shift my teaching toward skill building rather than content overloading; to provide additional opportunities for students to interact with each other and with me; to make positive use of student diversity and experience; and to more easily direct historical study toward areas of student interest and personal connection. Further, I wanted students to be increasingly engaged with primary and secondary sources that historians actually use. They would become historians themselves, engaged with the gold standard for historical research: original sources. I eliminated tests and integrated history problems in their place.

In format, the problems consist of three major pieces: a single-page contextual summary for the problem, problem questions (usually 4–6 multipart questions), and a variety of primary (and sometimes secondary) source materials that relate to the problem. A typical history problem packet is about 30 pages in length, inclusive of all of the pieces. Students have three to four weeks to work on the problems before submitting the written portion for evaluation. Each problem is created with the intention of developing historical thinking skills that are part of the five Cs (change over time, context, causality, complexity, and contingency) and creating dynamic classroom interaction around the respective problems.

Although class sessions are allocated to introduce the problem contextually, I am careful to not suggest or provide answers to the problems.

Instead, I facilitate discussions and debates that interact with the questions. An example of an in-class practice session with this is found in the following PowerPoint where students work together in class with a brief but complex problem involving geographic political representation before the Civil War (Figure 4.7). I want the students to wrestle with historical sources using the

Figure 4.7. Problem-based approach to historical thinking.

The Politics and Economics of Social Construction and Human Bondage

- **Question:** How is the number of state representatives to Congress determined?

- **Fact:** At the beginning of the United States, the White population in northern states is greater than in southern states.

- (**Problem:**) How can political power be made relatively equal between the two regions in a new national government?

- (**Solution?**) ———— A literal invitation for students to engage the problem

———— An early introduction to thinking about history in a problem-based manner (in terms of both content and analytic discipline-based method)

U.S. Population (estimated) –1790 Census

Color scheme:
Lightest map color = 2–6 persons per sq. mile

Midrange color = 18–45 persons per sq. mile

Darkest color = 90+ persons per sq. mile

Total U.S. pop . in 1790= estimated at 3.9 million (excluding Indians not-taxed)

Total slave pop. = approx. 700,000

Source: U.S. Census Bureau: https://www.census.gov/history/img/1790-b.jpg

Here we are introducing historical data but not providing a solution or answer to a problem. Space is being given for students to interpret meaning individually and in groups. This was not done in prior years. In prior courses I simply provided the interpretation and the answer.

elements of historical thinking and to do so with their classmates even while forming their own individual responses to the questions. I believe that students should have the same benefit as professional historians—to actively share their ideas, consider alternatives to their way of thinking, receive suggestions, and set to work on what they believe is a well-reasoned interpretation of the material. The history problems and class sessions surrounding them are intended to provide those opportunities.

As with my love of content, I need to be cautious in not making the history problems too large, too complex, or too many in number so as to resaturate the course with too much to cover. When I get enthusiastic about an idea, I tend to overdo. My enthusiasm for creating "history problems" ran full throttle in part because they seemed to resolve so many things that I found problematic in my teaching. For the first year of problem implementation, I developed six problems for the semester with a class of 75 students. Topics ranged from citizenship and voting rights for women in the 1870s to World War II and Americans of Japanese ancestry. Another problem focused on the challenges of "separate but equal" policies and the struggle involved in *Brown v. Board of Education* (1954), and yet another concentrated on the Cold War, 9/11, and the problems of containment. Even splitting the problems between the undergraduate teaching assistant and myself, we had 225 problems to grade. It buried us in paper as students frequently wrote 10 or more pages of responses. One student, a freshman, actually typed 20 to 25 pages per history problem. Also, the complexity of the problems caused the students to have to hurry through them to get ready for the next one. Students who use English as a second language found it difficult to translate the material into their native language and then express their responses in English again within such a short amount of time. It crowded the course schedule and caused undue fatigue for everyone.

With very good end-of-term advice from my teaching assistant and a colleague from my university's Center for Teaching and Learning, I scaled back the number of problems the following year. I am now using three history problems during a semester. That number proved wise as the course now has the breathing space to comfortably introduce and practice historical thinking skills, interact with a reasonable number of primary and secondary sources that span a respectable number of topics and time periods for a survey course, and for all students to experience the discipline of history as a practitioner.

As I continue to use history problems, new approaches to creating the problems emerge. This is consistent with our observation throughout this book about intercultural pedagogy being "in-process" and never fully complete. During the current semester (Spring 2016) I thought about how to more fully utilize the diverse perspectives of my students in creating a problem rather than providing them with a problem of my creation that related to their interests. I also wanted to find additional ways of meeting one of the main objectives of my course: having students experience being historians who interpret diverse primary sources. Combining problem creation with the experience of being historians was relatively easy and yet I had never done so in the course.

To change that, I used the final problem assignment to engage students in developing questions for a problem that focused on the Black Lives Matter movement. I also provided room for students to suggest sources in investigating the questions. The timing for doing this later in the semester was important given that students need familiarity and practice with the elements of historical thinking to develop effective questions that can be investigated. Further, it is useful to have developed some of the intercultural communication skills necessary to work effectively with peers while collaboratively developing the questions.

Including students in the process of developing questions and recommending sources for the Black Lives Matter history problem necessitated spending a portion of a two-hour class session revisiting historical thinking skills (context, change over time, causality, contingency, complexity—and now a sixth C that we as a class identified: consistency over time). Following this review, students broke into small groups of five students each to formulate questions regarding the Black Lives Matter movement and to identify some sources that would relate to the questions. The process worked well given that the questions that emerged were reflective of historical thinking skills *and* of the diverse perspectives of the students as they engaged one another. For example, the following questions emerged and were made part of the history problem:

- Using the sources available in this problem and from our class, what are some of the factors that led to and shaped the Black Lives Matter movement? How do these factors connect to and differ from other movements that we have studied? (These questions relate to causality, context, complexity, and consistency).
- What are the beliefs and guiding principles of the Black Lives Matter movement? What commonalities exist between these beliefs and principles and those of earlier movements? What differences exist?
- What are some of the strategies that the Black Lives Matter movement utilizes to achieve its goals? What are the strategic parallels and differences that we have studied?

In our conversations about these questions and the kinds of sources that could be used to investigate them, student perspectives emerged. For example, I found that students are interested in the origins of movements, what causes them to emerge, and how some remain many decades after their founding. In probing this further and thinking through what sources can inform these interests, students express admiration for the consistency of effective civil rights movements over time given their use of similar themes, the complex but largely parallel ways in which many are organized nationally and locally, and the strategic thinking that sustains their effectiveness. Students recommended that we look at statements of organizational founders to investigate questions involving causality and to utilize "official" websites to probe organizational beliefs and principles. By enabling students to contribute to the creation of a history problem, I was able to hear and utilize their perspectives; to further discover how they think about and use historical thinking skills; and to further place them in the role of being historians who design an historical investigation and identify the sources that relate to it.

I wondered how students were experiencing the problem-based approach to studying history and whether it was producing meaningful learning outcomes. With the support of a university teaching-related grant, I was able to engage an external evaluator to assess the use of history problems in my spring 2015 course. The student reactions were mostly very positive. The evaluator asked, "What parts of the course were particularly effective for you in developing historical thinking skills and the capacity to be an effective historian? What parts were particularly ineffective?" Representative student responses included the following:

- I enjoyed that we were able to learn and discuss the things that we decided on as a class, which made it more effective because people were more willing to learn. I think that allowing us to apply ourselves to our interests allowed us to look at history in a deeper and [more] intense way through learning historical thinking skills.
- The parts of this course that were effective in developing historical thinking skills were definitely the history problems and also the five Cs. I learned so much through the history problems that I would have never learned through a test and I will remember the information much better by writing about it in a history problem. I didn't feel like any part was ineffective.
- I think that the most effective things that we did in class to develop my historical thinking skills were definitely the problem sets and our class discussions. Both of those two platforms pushed us to think

for ourselves and contribute to a larger group discussion. I loved the problem sets because they forced me to think and form my own opinions using the historical thinking skills that we were given.

Although I still needed to make course adjustments, these were affirmations of the value of shifting my pedagogy toward a more interactive, problem-oriented approach where student voices emerged and collaborative thinking became more the norm. Still, I want to increasingly engage students by further tapping into their course-related interests, as they know them, and to make the course more personally relevant.

Invitation for Reflection

1. *How can I revise my teaching materials to invite and facilitate intercultural interactions and intellectual development within my discipline or field?*
2. *With whom can I consult or collaborate with professionally to review my course materials and offer informed suggestions for improvement in a manner consistent with the values of intercultural pedagogy?*

Discovering and Utilizing Student Interests and Experiences

> It is experience that shapes indigenous education and necessitates the awareness of self as crucial in order for knowledge to be attained. . . . Awareness of one's self is the beginning of learning. (Deloria & Wildcat, 2001, p. 13)

It is remarkable how much students will share when asked. This is particularly true when students know that what they share will be used respectfully. Like many things, I discovered this slowly. For years, I did not ask students about what interested them or try to connect learning with their lived experiences. By being pedagogically deaf I missed out on good teaching and learning opportunities. Now, in reflecting more deeply on my own best learning experiences, I recall that the most memorable teachers and educators that I encountered—persons like John Hope Franklin, Laura Rendón, and my undergraduate religion professor—held this in common: they strove to know with whom they were interacting and how to build early, respectful connections with them. This is so simple and yet so easily missed.

When I began asking students what they were interested in on the first day of my history course (as they introduced themselves to me and each other), it started a dialogue that proved fruitful. Slowly, as I incorporated their interests into the course design, content, assignments, and assessments, the process yielded more and more input from students. I worked from a simple catalog of what students told me and reaffirmed with my teaching assistant that what I heard was accurate. Together, we formed a basic listing as in the following from spring semester 2015 (the numbers in parentheses are the number of students who mentioned the topic specifically as one of interest. Topics without numbers were mentioned once. Some students did not know a particular interest on the first day of class):

WWII (6)
Civil rights (3)
Vietnam (2)
Great Depression (2)
1920s
Space Race
Other countries and perceptions of the United States
Native Americans and tribes
Immigrants
Civil War and differing economies
Romanov family
1950s

To further probe and understand these initial interests, I gave students a very brief paper survey on the first day of class. The survey asks questions about how students believe they learn best, the attributes of the best courses they ever took, and their historical interests to the extent that they know them. This survey yields high response rates (generally 90%–100%), and I discover much more about the students and their diverse interests and perspectives as a result.

A few examples from last semester help to demonstrate the depth of some initial interests and how they intersect with personal experience and multicultural histories. One student returned the survey with her expression of strong interest in

> The Vietnam War. My grandparents and parents lived through that harsh time period. Not only that, I want others to know that Hmong people were forced into battle against Laotians, Vietnamese, etc. (it is also called "The Secret War") and that is why we, the Hmong people, have no land and are promised and brought to the U.S. to have better lives.

Another student from the same class shared that much of his early life was lived in Vietnam and that he wanted to know more about the Vietnam War as well as about the Great Depression. These students, and others in the course, provided rich insight—infused with personal connections that they shared—into how the course could be formed to engage their interests and experiences. Given the requested input from the students, I made absolutely certain that these topics would be discussed in class and would be approached in a way that was inclusive of their interpretations and voices. We did so through collaborative question development so that students could practice and use historical questioning to guide our inquiry with historical sources.

In our study of Vietnam, students (including the two students noted earlier) generated questions about why the United States became involved in the war (causality) as well as why the "secret war" was necessary, why it was secret, and why it involved the Hmong people so heavily (which involved context, complexity, change over time, and contingency). Other questions on the war in Vietnam concerned probing the contexts, politics, and philosophies of those led by Ho Chi Minh in Vietnam's northern region. These questions created a wonderfully complex study of what Americans call the Vietnam War, but we discovered the cultural and geographic complexities of a conflict that was much larger, longer, and costlier (in human life) than that.

Students were able to research these questions and interpret the histories associated with this conflict in a manner that gave space to their voice and what they wished to share. Without prompting from me, some students called attention to Hmong art that emerged from the war depicting the sacrifice of Hmong people and villages as a result of fighting in the war on behalf of the United States. Another student mentioned an opportunity to go see Hmong art and artifacts at a local exhibit. Still others shared family stories of displacement and movement from Laos, to Thailand, and on to the United States. It was incredibly rich engagement by the full class, sparked by the particular interests of a few students that enabled us to engage in a powerful, multiculturally informed study of the past while simultaneously developing historical thinking skills.

In another class, we studied conceptions about the idea of the "American Dream" and how the idea or phrase emerged historically and whether it held any of its original meaning with Americans today. I asked students to investigate contemporary expressions of the American Dream—or criticisms of it—and to write a brief interpretive paper about what they found. One of the students, Andrea, found it to be a powerful way to connect familial experience with historical study.

One assignment I enjoyed was interviewing a person about understanding the American Dream. I interviewed my mother so she could tell me about her experiences immigrating to America. This assignment made me feel I have a valuable story to tell about my family roots and feel confident that I was different from others but important. After the class, I volunteered to talk in panels for Latino parents that were seeking information about their sons and daughters coming to the university. I could relate to them because I am a first-generation college student from an immigrant family. Now, I feel more confident about myself and that I am an important part for this society.

When first creating this assignment, I had no preconceptions about the powerful outcomes that it would produce. But it reinforced for me as a historian and as an emergent practitioner of intercultural pedagogy that there is great benefit in bringing together student interests and experience in the study of history. Andrea's experience and those of other students pushed me forward in connecting history to lived experience.

The great benefits derived from hearing students and what they contribute to the complexity of historical inquiry and multicultural interpretations of the past caused me to further modify my method of assessing their work as historians. The most recent modification is not a new technique among many of my colleagues, but it was new for me in developing greater insight into how students process historical information beyond what they share in writing.

Invitation for Reflection

1. *How can I solicit student interests that are relevant to my course?*
2. *How can I connect course content to student experiences and interests?*
3. *How can I connect student experience and interests to course assignments?*

Diversifying the Assessment of Learning

The problem-posing educator constantly re-forms his reflections in the reflection of the students. The students—no longer docile listeners—are now critical co-investigators in dialogue with the teacher. The teacher presents the material to the students for their consideration, and re-considers her earlier considerations as the students express their own. (Freire, 1970, pp. 61–62)

Rich disciplinary and cultural interactions with students in the classroom as well as during individual meetings in my office made me think about modifying how I assess their work as historians. Since the beginning of my undergraduate teaching experience, I relied entirely on assessing written responses to test questions and, later, history problems. Earlier in this chapter, I described the way that I deepened the complexity of assessment, yet without diversifying the types of assessments I was integrating into the course. During study review sessions for tests or open discussion sessions with students about the history problems, I heard wonderfully insightful interpretations, ideas, and cultural values that many times never found expression in their papers. With an interest in assessing their knowledge, skills, and ideas as comprehensively as possible, I decided to add a verbal component to the assessment of history problems.

As I mentioned earlier, I have many international students who use English as a second or even a third language. In interpersonal interactions with them, they sometimes find it easier to communicate ideas verbally than in writing. Frequently, we assess the difficult written interpretive work of students for whom English is a second language as if they were completely fluent in our language. (Imagine, for just a moment, if the tables were turned. How well could I, for example, respond in Mandarin to a complex history problem on the Yuan Dynasty?) Although it is important to provide comment on how to express ideas with greater clarity and to facilitate growth in using English (which we do through extensive comments), it is very important to think clearly about the priorities for assessing assignments such as history problems. I do not prioritize grammar or written work alone; instead, I want to read *and* hear how students approach history problems using historical thinking skills, what they find most challenging in doing so, and to give students opportunities for verbally clarifying unclear portions of their writing. Essentially, this mimics the processes that many of us as professional scholars go through when engaging our own challenging scholarship.

To facilitate this process and yet make it manageable, I scheduled a 15- to 20-minute individual appointments with students over 2 weeks after the first and third history problems. During the appointments we focus on clarifying or further describing their written response to the paper that they submitted. Students know that they can earn some additional points for clarifications and that they cannot lose any points as a result of the meeting. This provides excellent opportunity to hear more from the students and how they thought about primary sources and used them, and what they found challenging in working with the history problem. Students also provide me with feedback about the structure of the problem and the sources, and what would make working with the problem more effective (e.g., additional context setting in class, clarifications about the wording of the problem questions). The conversations, along with the written responses, give me a good sense of how well each student is mastering the components of historical thinking and where I need to spend more time in class clarifying a particular thinking skill (e.g., I found many students have difficulty understanding the idea of contingency in history).

Even on days when I could meet with as many as 12 students (with some breaks built in between meetings), I found that the meetings went quickly and that I genuinely enjoyed them. What I gained from investing this time with individual students was a better understanding of how they approached and utilized historical information, where they encountered challenges in interpreting historical information, and where they found that they *could* incorporate their own voices and interests. This information enabled me to continue to revise the class and to revisit historical thinking skill development areas that seemed most challenging or unclear to students.

Meeting with students individually about their responses to history problems also produces an environment where students can engage me as cohistorians and scholars and where we can collaboratively challenge the meaning of sources or assumptions within our interpretations. There are special moments when students ask highly advanced questions that challenge my own thoughts about a particular source and its context. Historian G. R. Elton (1967) spoke of this kind of interaction in his book, *The Practice of History*:

> I remember many occasions on which attempts to explain something to a student suddenly brought into focus the components of a problem, for the first time showed me where accepted interpretations had been too easily accepted, or by making me think afresh made me reorganize a mass of material of which the student, the stimulus to it all, could not even be aware. (p. 143)

There are moments too when students will infuse within their interpretations of sources cultural values that are fascinating to read and hear. Our conversations stimulate such cultural encounters. One such time occurred when one of my students from South Korea commented on a personal outcome on completing a challenging history problem on life within Jim Crow systems of oppression. He observed that in reading about the multiple injustices directed toward African Americans within Jim Crow society, he felt greater compassion for people and a commitment to justice for all persons who suffer injustice. For him, it was a moral outcome situated within what he identified as a cultural value of responsible ethical behavior toward others and the responsibility to seek social justice. I was pleased that his voice and cultural nuances came through in our meeting and also within some of his writing. I encouraged continuation of cultural expression and sharing within his writing and through personal interactions. My prior forms of assessments—such as the test formats that I used—would not have encouraged this and, likely, this student's voice would have been voided by memorization and the dominance of my voice. How we assess student learning and thinking affects greatly the alignment present or absent in our intercultural pedagogy.

Invitation for Reflection

1. *What are my current methods of assessing student knowledge and skills? Are my assessment methods consistent with disciplinary practices of learning, discovering, and expressing knowledge?*
2. *How can I assess student learning in ways that honor and utilize the diversity of my students and their different ways of expressing knowledge?*

Conclusion

My journey toward intercultural pedagogy within the discipline of history is a slow but steady progression full of experimentation, revision, failures and missed opportunities, further revisions—large and small—and very gratifying successes. It is propelled by a genuine desire to engage students in collaborative investigation of the past where the thrill of discovery and meaning-making is fully present and where their voices and experiences are valued and seamlessly integrated within the learning process. The best teachers that I ever had did the same.

Many of those teachers were outside of my disciplinary area and I wondered if I could engage intercultural pedagogy within the disciplinary standards of historical thinking. I believe that it is possible and that our professional practices as historians closely align with the attributes of intercultural pedagogy. Historians value the diverse voices of those who experienced life with differing perspectives, experiences, and epistemologies. They add to our understanding of the past and the cultural complexities that are part of the distant and more contemporary historical record. Our interactions with professional peers increase our awareness of the craft of historical inquiry and sharpen our thinking. So too can students, if we trust in their ability to generate understanding and knowledge through use of relevant experience, skillfully facilitated classroom interactions, well-designed assignments, and well-assessed learning.

5

CASE STUDY

Catherine

Critical theorists urge teachers and learners to continually "unlearn," "learn," "relearn," "reflect," and "evaluate," going beneath the surface to understand context, ideology, discourse, and actions (Shor, 1999). In my research practice, I find this a wonderful challenge that is integral to the discovery of new knowledge. It is a bit more challenging, though, to be "critical" in my teaching—to create learning environments that engage students to collaborate with me in those same processes, to go to places of vulnerability and share ideas, feelings, and insights with almost-strangers who happen to occupy the same classroom space at a given point in time.

The challenge is exacerbated by the lack of a definitive road map for navigating those conditions and relationships to create authentic intercultural learning. There was a point in time, not too long ago, when the primary tools I used to develop my courses were a varying combination of disciplinary norms, colleagues' syllabi for similar courses, personal experience, and intuition. When the norms of my discipline and the ways courses like mine have been previously taught did not align with my own experiences of developing intercultural sensitivity, I was left to a trial and error process. Although there is a place for each of these aspects in educational design, they are not the best preconditions for the type of intentional intercultural learning I wanted to foster in my classroom. It was based on this realization, as well as the affirmation and support of like-minded colleagues who helped me stretch to think more critically and deeply, that I began an intentional journey of unlearning, learning, relearning, reflecting, and evaluating. It is in this spirit that I invite you to learn with me as I share critical (and ongoing) pivot points in the development of my intercultural pedagogy.

Working With Tensions

Reflecting on how my teaching evolved over a 10-year period, I recall tensions, the discomfort they produced, the pedagogical decisions they necessitated, and the changes I made in my courses. The following sections describe the macro- and micro-adjustments that I made to the Global and Diverse Families course. As a whole, it is a process of gaining awareness and alignment—specifically, aligning the course objectives, strategies, and assessments while simultaneously aligning the course design with my intentions and intercultural approach. In reality, however, it was less linear than that. The decisions and resulting actions described in the following narrative did not occur in a neat, logical order; rather, they were made, tested, evaluated, and refined over several semesters. I present what happened ahead more or less in the chronological order in which it occurred for me; I have done so as proof that there are many entry points into this work and ways of developing a course that embodies an intercultural pedagogy.

In the first semester that I taught the Global and Diverse Families course, I was quite disappointed to note a pattern reflected in learners' presentations and essays—a radical reduction of the complexity of the family system, regardless of the students' culture of origin. They used broad categories to describe families within an identified culture and compared and contrasted them to families in other cultures. They presented family relationships and processes in static and mono-dimensional ways. The following brief examples typify the writing that learners frequently submitted that first semester:

> Culture A is collectivist, which means the group or the family is of primary importance. That is one of the reasons they care for elders at home. This is different from elders in Culture B, which is individualistic. When Culture B elders need care, they are placed in nursing homes until the end of life.

OR

> Marriages are based on love in Culture A but are arranged in Culture B.

OR

> Families in Culture A are Buddhist so they believe in reincarnation.

Although there is value in having a sense of some of the general characteristics of a given culture, that should be the starting point to understanding families in that culture. It should not be the endpoint of the analysis or, more importantly, the endpoint of a learner's attempt to understand the differences within and among families. Yet I was not seeing evidence that learners were able to think about culture and families in more complex ways. In class we discussed the variation within and across cultures, as well as the dynamic nature of families and cultures over time, particularly due to forces of globalization that are often inextricably linked to families' intercultural identities, yet learners were not internalizing those ideas.

At first, my frustration led me to conclude that I was an ineffective teacher. Somehow learners were just not getting what I thought I was teaching. But then I spent some time reflecting on the readings, films, and assignments I had inherited for the course to try to understand the root of this disconnection. It did not take long to figure it out: course materials generally framed family and culture in similar monolithic, static ways and used broad categories to compare and contrast across cultural groups. My teaching approach aligned with the course, but the course itself was the problem. The course was not aligned with—nor did it reflect—how I personally developed interculturally, how I interacted with culturally diverse others, and what I felt was important for future family professionals to know. Herein lay a deep tension that I needed to acknowledge and work to resolve.

Table 5.1 highlights five tensions that represent the impetus for developing an intercultural pedagogy as they relate to my Global and Diverse Families course. I envision these tensions along a continuum, running left to right.

TABLE 5.1
Five Core Tensions

Tension between . . .		
Content mastery—knowing about culturally diverse families	. . . and . . .	Process—knowing *how to learn about and interact with* culturally diverse families
Cultural simplicity—knowing that families in a particular culture behave in an expected pattern	. . . and . . .	Cultural variation—understanding that there is considerable family variation within cultures due to intersections with other social locations, such as race, class, and gender
Cultural stability—assuming cultures remain static over time	. . . and . . .	Cultural dynamism—understanding that cultures change and adapt over time
Considering differences of "others"	. . . and . . .	Considering differences of "another"
Cultural competence and confidence—I have mastered facts about cultural attributes so therefore I know	. . . and . . .	Cultural humility—knowing what you don't know and being open to ongoing learning through interaction

In each set of tensions described, the left side represents my perception of the norm in my discipline. The syllabus and the text/readings I inherited focused on knowing family characteristics of distinct cultural groups, understanding families through a monolithic cultural lens, and noting similarities and differences in families across cultures. The gist of this approach was that if learners could master a specified body of knowledge about families in diverse cultures, our graduates would be culturally competent.

The right side reflects how I think about families and culture. I seek to have learners understand how the experience of family is shaped by culture. I try to focus particularly on the variations of family experience within and across cultures, the dynamic nature of families across time and space, that it is problematic to default to a Western family prototype as the norm to which all other families are compared, and that intercultural learning is an ongoing process of engagement.

The tensions are highly interconnected, but the first tension drives the rest. With a pedagogical focus on content mastery, learners are taught to simplistically categorize cultures by attributes that can be compared across cultural boundaries. These are often presented as dichotomous: individual/collectivist, matriarchal/patriarchal, large families/small families, arranged marriages/love marriages. A mastery approach also fixes these characteristics of families in one point in time, ignoring how influences of globalization, migration, political upheavals, natural disasters, and technology are continually changing families throughout the world. If caution is not taken, a content mastery approach can reinforce Western privilege, locating White middle-class families as the norm and noting difference in terms of that referent. Finally, knowing "about" can lead learners to a false sense of "competence" as they develop "expertise" about a particular culture but lack the ability to interact with anyone who is from that same culture.

Although I was clear that I was not comfortable teaching to the left anchor of the tension continuum, I was less clear about how I could move learners to the right anchor. Initially I was hesitant to pay attention to it. My training as a researcher told me to push it into the background, to be objective, to follow disciplinary norms, to continue on the path using the syllabus that had been handed to me by predecessors. It was a required course, approved at some point in time and deemed essential for our majors to take. The university had also approved it as a course that met the global awareness liberal education standard. Moreover, I received great teaching evaluations! Learners loved learning "about" families from different cultures. My "don't fix it if it isn't broken" reaction is an example of what Katila and colleagues (2010) described as "habituated modes of practice." I was acquiescing to forces that reinforced the status quo—a disciplinary approach to teaching in this content area, a departmental practice of approving courses and expecting them to be consistently taught over time, an institutional set of "quality" standards for good teaching by which faculty are evaluated, evidenced by student evaluations.

Considering all of that, it would have been much easier to continue with the current syllabus and teach the course in the same way. Yet I knew that I could not maintain the status quo and replicate practice that did not facilitate the learning I felt our graduates needed to be successful as global citizens and family science professionals. My discomfort and instinct indicated that something needed to change. So I took Katila and colleagues' (2010) Step 2—I started to question my pedagogy, my practice of teaching. Then I took Step 3—I began to search for new teaching and learning strategies that would facilitate the development of learners' intercultural interacting abilities that are necessary to effectively navigate an increasingly complex cultural world. And so the experimentation process began.

Moving from an approach that reinforced the left anchors on the tension continuum to one that enacted the right anchors involved a series of decisions, designs, and adjustments. I was clear about what was not effective, so it was easier to make decisions to eliminate certain aspects of the course. I was less clear, however, about what would replace them. I had to be okay with experimenting with new learning activities and the accompanying feelings of uncertainty about whether they would result in the outcomes I was hoping to achieve. I also needed to commit to this as ongoing processes of trial and error, of observing learners' engagement, and of listening to learners' feedback. What follows here are steps I took to revise my course to better align it with my intercultural pedagogy.

Step 1: Creating Learning Objectives That Reflected an Intercultural Pedagogy

Step 1 in my process involved critically examining the existing learning objectives in the course. I retained some of them because they were currently on record for meeting liberal education requirements at my institution. I added new objectives that better reflected my intercultural pedagogy. That required that I delete some excellent existing objectives that I felt were of less priority and couldn't be addressed effectively due to time constraints. Table 5.2 shows the final list of objectives that guide student learning in my course.

TABLE 5.2
Revised Learning Objectives

Learning Objectives
• Demonstrate a basic understanding of family life of people in various cultures around the world (existing)
• Demonstrate awareness of important global family issues (existing)
• Identify how culture influences individuals' experiences of family (new)
• Respect different ways to experience family across and within cultural groups (new)
• Apply a human ecology framework to analyze the role of culture in human service organizations that serve diverse families in the Twin Cities and the families they serve (new)
• Use human ecology concepts to compare and contrast family experiences globally (new)
• Evaluate one's own location on the intercultural development continuum (new)
• Learn to suspend judgment by recognizing how one's own values, roles, beliefs, traditions, lifestyles, and understanding of family may impact interactions with families from cultures different than one's own (new)
• Critically reflect on one's privileges and how they impact multicultural interactions (new)
• Identify opportunities to expand one's cultural and global awareness (new)

Step 2: Creating Pedagogically Aligned Assignments

The existing course's major research assignment required learners to conduct library research and create a presentation on family life in a specific culture. This was not in any way congruent with the intercultural pedagogy I was developing. In fact, it was one of the major culprits in leading learners to be confident that they knew "about" families in a variety of cultures. For several years I agonized over dropping an assignment used in the course. What would be an equivalent replacement? What types of assignments would help learners apply the important ideas in the course? At the point I dropped the assignment, I had no clear idea about what I would create to replace it. But I was clear that it was working at odds with my goals for student learning.

After two semesters with no major assignment in the course, I created a digital ethno-narrative assignment. The primary learning goal for this assignment was that students would learn to recognize and respect the many and varied ways to experience family within and across cultures. This explicitly addressed the first tension, learning "about" families versus learning how to learn about families. Teams of two to three learners identify a key informant from a culture different than their own, conduct basic library research to gather initial facts about their key informant's country/culture of origin and any family characteristics that have been documented in literature, and draft an interview protocol based on that research. I review the interview drafts and provide extensive feedback before they conduct the interview. Interviews are videotaped and the teams garner written permission to share the videos. I am clear with learners that this is the key informant's story, not theirs. Their job is to ask excellent questions that elicit good information, to capture that on video, and to respectfully edit the video to communicate their key informant's story about how culture shapes his or her experience of family.

Through the use of this digital ethno-narrative assignment, learners accomplish the following goals: (a) they are effective in demonstrating diversity within and across cultures; (b) they embody culture as a dynamic idea—there are often key informants that represent two generations in a culture, and change over time and space becomes quite clear; (c) they demonstrate that key informants are effective teachers about culture through their sharing of common and diverse experiences of family; and (d) they facilitate qualitative research skill development, including conducting library research, writing interview questions, conducting and videotaping interviews, conducting thematic analysis, and synthesizing themes. I felt that I was getting closer to addressing a number of the tensions I had originally seen in the course. An example from a learner's response to a final question demonstrates her understanding of complexity, diversity, and the dynamic nature of culture:

> Clearly, these two stories show that common cultural themes can shape families in very different ways. In addition, globalization has affected all families around the world, creating many people with bicultural identities, as I saw with Chria and Ahmed, but globalization has also affected how I understand other people's cultures. With more diverse peoples moving to my community and with the readily available information due to globalization, I can understand more cultures and through this understanding, be able to relate better to friends and family.

In the previous chapter, Bob described freeing himself from the "tyranny of content" by cutting lecture material. Similarly, removing an ineffective, time-consuming project from the Global and Diverse Families course provided the space to create and implement a learning activity that allowed for more cultural discovery and meaningful development.

The digital ethno-narrative assignment is only one example of an assignment I created to achieve the new intercultural pedagogy–aligned learning

objectives in my course. I actually had to delete/revise/add several assignments as well as assessments (assessments will be addressed later in the chapter). As I went through this process, it was critical for me to continually
return to my learning objectives to check for alignment. Table 5.3 reflects
that alignment.

TABLE 5.3
Mapping Learning Strategies and Assessment to Revised Objectives

Learning Objective	Learning Strategies and Assessment
Demonstrate a basic understanding of family life of people in various cultures around the world (existing)	**Strategies:** Key informant digital ethno-narratives **Assessment:** Analysis and synthesis of narratives; final synthesis paper
Demonstrate awareness of important global family issues (existing)	**Strategies:** Textbook readings, films, speakers **Assessment:** Film analysis; speaker reflections; online discussions; final synthesis paper
Identify how culture influences individuals' experiences of family (new)	**Strategies:** Personal culture digital stories; key informant digital ethno-narratives **Assessment:** Analysis and synthesis of themes in peers' stories and key informants' narratives
Respect different ways to experience family across and within cultural groups (new)	**Strategies:** Personal culture digital stories; key informant digital ethno-narratives **Assessment:** Final synthesis paper
Apply a human ecology framework to analyze the role of culture in human service organizations that serve diverse families in the Twin Cities and the families these organizations serve (new)	**Strategies:** 24 hours of service-learning—volunteering in local nonprofit agencies **Assessment:** Service-learning journal reflections
Use human ecology concepts to compare and contrast family experiences globally (new)	**Strategies:** Films, speakers, digital ethno-narratives **Assessment:** Online reflections; digital ethno-narrative analysis and synthesis

(Continues)

TABLE 8.3 *(Continued)*

Learning Objective	Learning Strategies and Assessment
Evaluate one's own location on the intercultural development continuum (new)	**Strategies:** "Frame" exercise, class discussion, service-learning experiences **Assessment:** Reflection paper (self-assessment); final synthesis paper (growth over time)
Learn to suspend judgment by recognizing how one's own values, roles, beliefs, traditions, lifestyles, and understanding of family may impact interactions with families from cultures different than one's own (new)	**Strategies:** Service-learning **Assessment:** Service-learning journal reflections (self-assessment) and in-class debriefing; online discussion forums; final synthesis paper
Critically reflect on one's privileges and how they impact multicultural interactions (new)	**Strategies:** Service-learning **Assessment:** Service-learning journal reflections (self-assessment); final synthesis paper
Identify opportunities to expand one's cultural and global awareness (new)	**Strategies:** Service-learning journal reflections **Assessment:** Final synthesis (self-assessment)

Invitation for Reflection

With your course syllabus in hand, consider the following questions as you examine your learning objectives, making notes on your syllabus:

1. *Thinking about the values of intercultural pedagogy, how are these demonstrably evident in your syllabus/course design?*
2. *Which learning objectives clearly articulate the types of intercultural learning and values that you want to occur in your class? Identify the ones that align and the ones that don't align.*
3. *How can you address and revise nonaligning objectives? Should they be deleted or revised?*
4. *How does the course syllabus explicitly communicate priorities? How does the syllabus implicitly convey learning priorities? (In both cases, pay close attention to how you allocate class time, how you ask students to invest out-of-class time, and how assignments and activities are weighted.)*
5. *Does the syllabus communicate how diversity will be valued by and relevant to the learning process? If not, how and where can this be incorporated in substantive ways?*

Step 3: Adding a Theoretical Lens to Encourage Complex Thinking

To address the second tension of oversimplification of culture, I needed to add complexity to learners' thinking about families and culture. To start this process, I introduced learners to a human ecological framework (Figure 5.1) (Bubolz & Sontag, 1993) that requires them to consider multiple contextual layers that influence the experience of family, of which "culture" is one of many. The framework considers nested environments that shape human interaction—*the human-built environment* (infrastructure; e.g., homes, schools, roads), *the sociocultural environment* (culture, values, attitudes, beliefs, behaviors, relationships, economic/political/religious systems, etc.), and *the natural physical environment* (climate, rivers, forests, etc.). I refer to this model regularly throughout the semester, and several assignments require students to use the framework to describe what they are observing.

The use of these lenses creates an intentionality around learners' consideration of cultural identity formation as they use it to frame their personal cultural story and in other aspects of the course, as well. By consciously "peeling back the layers of the onion," they begin to see how their environments and experiences, resulting in a more complex understanding of self, have uniquely shaped them. It then becomes a bit easier to consider how others have been similarly or differently shaped by their unique set of environments and experiences.

Figure 5.1. Human ecology framework.

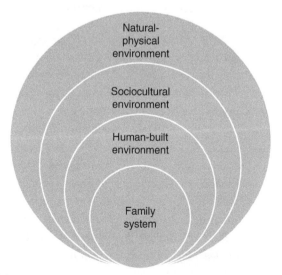

Natural-
physical
environment

Sociocultural
environment

Human-built
environment

Family
system

Note. Bubolz and Sontag (1993).

A learner's writing reflects that inward discovery and outward application:

> Throughout this course, I learned a lot that affirmed my personal identity, including my beliefs, values, and cultural identity. When creating my personal cultural story, I had a fun time examining my culture and looking at how my family, friends, and environment impacted me. This project really affirmed my personal identity, including how I understand my own culture and how I am embedded in different systems from the ecological model. In addition, learning about my own culture made me curious about other cultures, and I really enjoyed watching other personal culture stories to compare them to my own.

Step 4: Increasing Awareness and Expression of My Pedagogical Approach

It was fortuitous that as I experienced the tensions discussed at the beginning of this chapter and struggled to make sense of them, I participated in my university's Internationalizing Teaching and Learning faculty cohort program. The initiative is organized by the university's central international office and is part of a broader initiative to support faculty in efforts to internationalize the curriculum and to ensure that all students are exposed to global, international, and intercultural learning in on-campus courses. My participation in this program legitimized taking the time to consciously examine and reflect on my course and make the needed changes. I was supported through the process by experts in intercultural learning and internationalizing curricula as well as by fellow sojourner colleagues—my community of practice. Both the time and the community were helpful to me.

As I read about the process of developing intercultural awareness and skills and the pedagogy of intercultural practice, my unconscious course design began to come into focus. First, I became keenly aware that I think about culture and families from a social constructivist lens rather than a positivist perspective. My paradigm is that one's reality is constructed by interactions with others, is shaped by our experiences, and is highly contextual. My lens aligns well with the right anchors of the tensions I identified. Bringing this to conscious attention explained why I was not comfortable teaching to the left anchors.

Second, I realized several threads were woven through the course: (a) globalization and its impact on families, (b) culture—how it shapes families and intercultural interacting; and (c) social justice. I intuitively understood how the threads connected to one another, but learners were experiencing the semester as disjointed. Once I articulated the three threads, I created a visual to introduce course objectives, course design, and course activities and assignments (Figure 5.2).

Figure 5.2. Visual of three interwoven course threads.

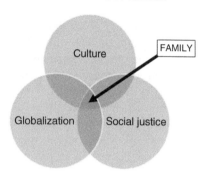

I use the visual throughout the semester to highlight the thread or threads that are being addressed and help learners make connections among various aspects of the course. The visual also helps me more clearly articulate the focus and the integration. For example, in past semesters, we had great class discussions about global trends and issues that were impacting families globally. We also had important sessions during which learners debriefed their service-learning experiences. Yet the two were not connected for them until I consciously created space for that connective thinking by posting a question in our online forum: *Your text and our guest speaker discussed a global issue of international violence that displaces families and creates long-lasting individual and family trauma. You also shared in class tonight about your local experiences in your service-learning sites. Write your reflection about how those two (global and local) are connected AND why it's important to make that connection in today's interconnected world.*

A learner's response suggests that those connections are being made:

Global and local issues I think are highly intertwined with each other because it almost represents the butterfly effect. Although I see many diverse people at my volunteer site and they have their own problems and adversities, it all trickles down from larger-scale problems. For example, I work with people that are from different countries and do not know English fluently. They are learning to navigate in this country because for some reason, they did not want to be in their home country anymore. Regarding what we talked about today, many people seek asylum and refuge when they come to America. For all I know, the families I am working with could have fled their country for various unsafe reasons. On a global scale, places like Syria are struggling for survival. This comes back to being on a local scale because once they move, they will still face the adversities that come with living in a new country as a refugee. I think it's important to understand this connection so that we as humans can do our best job to help as many people as we can in need.

Step 5: Moving Assessment From Exam to Synthesis

As I proceeded to incorporate new assignments that fit my emerging intercultural pedagogy, I realized that I had not considered how I would evaluate student learning on a final exam in this new learning context. Using Fink's (2003) model of course design for significant learning, the central course design process we used in the Internationalizing Teaching and Learning cohort, I asked myself this question: "What impact do I want this course experience to have on students that will still be there a year or more after taking this course?" (p. 75). In my cohort community of practice, it prompted us to think less about specific competencies and more about the longer-term impact we hope our intercultural pedagogy can generate. So I asked myself some questions to stimulate my thinking: How will I know that a learner has grasped these ideas? Are there language cues? Are there nonverbal cues? How do we discern whether learners are talking the talk versus walking the walk? Is self-reflection a valid form of assessment? I knew that ideas of complexity, dynamic change, variation, and interactions introduced did not lend themselves to multiple-choice questions. As a result, I "transgressed" in hooks (1994) language by not giving a final exam but assessing learning via a "final synthesis." I decided to try this approach despite feelings that colleagues might deem it less than "rigorous," that learners wouldn't take it seriously, and that I would struggle to effectively evaluate what they wrote.

The first question of the final synthesis introduced a case study describing an intercultural interaction between an international student and a professor that went awry. Learners were asked to identify what cultural values and worldviews may have been in conflict and how that led to misunderstanding. They were also asked to identify ways that each party might have improved the intercultural interaction to reduce the chance of misunderstanding. A second question asked learners to use the human ecology framework to describe and illustrate the complexity and discuss the impact on families of a situation in one of the films that dealt with armed conflict, political oppression, or government policies. A third question asked learners to locate themselves in M. J. Bennett's (1993) developmental model of intercultural sensitivity (DMIS), discuss why they placed themselves in that developmental stage, and suggest ways that they might engage in activities that would help them to move further along the continuum from ethnocentrism to ethno-relativism. A fourth question asked them to identify three key informants from the digital ethno-narratives, describe at least three themes in each narrative, providing specifics about how they demonstrated cultural influences on the experience of family, and then compare and contrast the three narratives, noting similarities and differences. A fifth question asked learners to share a reflection about something in one of the films, speaker presentations, or peer-peer or learner-instructor interactions that challenged some aspect of their personal identity (e.g., race, class, culture, age, sexual orientation, religion). They were asked to describe the situation, what was challenged, their reaction to it, how they dealt with it, and what they learned from their discomfort. I evaluated the final synthesis papers on learners' ability to articulate key concepts, think critically about situations that involved intercultural interactions, be self-reflective about their own intercultural development, and demonstrate complexity in their understanding of families and culture. I was pleased to see evidence of all of those outcomes to at least some extent.

Here are a few examples of what learners wrote:

(Student Response 1) For example, through watching the digital ethno-narratives, I have a deeper understanding of how culture impacts families' beliefs, values, gender roles, etc. By having this cultural understanding, I will be able to relate to the families I work with and be able to forget the judgments and stereotypes I may have originally had about the culture. These videos have shown me that just because you come from the same country, culture does not affect all families in the same way.

(Student Response 2) One experience that challenged me over the course of this semester was in one of the cultural narratives. It was when Abeba from Ethiopia was talking about how she still expects to receive a dowry from the man she will marry. This was difficult for me because it challenges what I view in terms of feminism, and I view that idea as subordination of women in general. I took my discomfort in the situation as an opportunity to see it from another's perspective. She mentioned that for her, a lot of what she liked about it had to do with respect. For me, the reason I consider myself a feminist is because I want an equal amount of respect that's given to men. Basically, it made me realize that my view of what she had said may have been a little skewed, and I jumped to negative conclusions too quickly. I learned that different cultures have different ways of showing respect, and that's okay.

(Student Response 3) I think specifically during Mohamed's digital narrative I felt my personal beliefs being challenged. His views on gender roles and gender equality are drastically different from what I view equality to be. It is often hard for me sometimes to listen to and engage with culturally diverse groups of people who do not have the same values as I do when it comes to gender roles. This value is so closely tied to my personal identity,

I think it can hinder my learning when it comes to cultural and diversity studies. In this particular case, I brought my thoughts to light in class. I was able to think about how it made me feel, and it's something I'm still thinking about because I need to separate my identity from other values and beliefs in order to be culturally sensitive and understanding. This, for me, is a continuing process.

(Student Response 4) When we discussed historical trauma and applied it to current warfare, I was challenged as an American Indian to understand that historical trauma is not only an isolated incidence for American Indians, but rather an incident that happens to many different cultures globally.

(Student Response 5) Something that challenged my beliefs that I heard from a peer when doing the mate selection activity was that she didn't believe in marriage. She has a kid and a steady boyfriend but does not believe in the idea of marriage. This shocked me because most people in American culture seem to believe in marriage. I didn't really know what to think but it forced me to think about how life has shaped her. I was definitely confused at first. But I have learned that even though it makes me uncomfortable, I should evaluate why it does. It really made me realize that just because someone looks and seems like they are in your culture, doesn't mean they have the same beliefs and values as you.

Invitation for Reflection

Heeding Fink's (2013) advice, pause and focus on the effectiveness of your assessment measures; do not jump straight into a review of the learning activities and teaching methods that you like and that students enjoy. It is easy to justify the inclusion of these based on satisfaction, but this process is designed to ensure that those activities and methods are the most effective at helping you achieve your learning goals.

1. *Are the assessments you are using (or have in mind) effective in demonstrating students' progress toward developing the knowledge, openness, and interpersonal skills that form the foundation of an intercultural pedagogy?*
2. *Do your assessments focus on demonstrating concrete, acquired knowledge or do they allow for reflection and demonstration of ongoing learning?*
3. *Have you made decisions about where to assign grades and where to provide ungraded feedback for intercultural learning?*

Once you have explored your assessment measures (and it may take a while), do an inventory of the learning objects, materials, readings, ways of using time in class, assignments, and activities that you use in your course. This is where it will be helpful to use the materials that you have gathered to also ensure that what you are outlining in the course syllabus matches with the learning objects that students encounter in the course. There are a number of things to consider, but suggested places to focus your attention include:

4. *Do you want learners to consider diverse perspectives? If so, where is this reflected and available in your content selections? In your assignments? Readings?*
5. *Does the syllabus explicitly communicate about the classroom environment? If so, what does it communicate about the qualities and values that will inform interactions or about the climate you aspire to establish? Does it support intercultural pedagogy?*
6. *How do you allocate time in the course design? Does the way you ask students to invest time in class and doing homework reflect the values of intercultural pedagogy, or does it emphasize teaching to and learning content? Is there flexibility in this?*
7. *Do the assignments and our assessments of student learning align with what we profess we want students to learn and enact? Are the assignments and assessments in dissonance with one another and in need of alignment?*

Expertise Is Fluid and Developmental: Revision and Reflection Are Key Practices to Enacting This Idea

As I worked through revisions to my course—learning objectives, assignments, assessments—I also became very aware of the importance of creating a climate in students' learning environment that would foster interaction, be equitable and inclusive, and be safe to openly share thoughts and ideas without judgment. I offer here reflections and experiences that illustrate my ongoing development as a teacher who strives to enact an intercultural pedagogy.

Pursuing Equity and Inclusion in Classrooms

Sensitivity to equity and inclusion is demanded in a course that focuses on families, which is a social construction that is deeply embedded in and shaped by culture. My own experience of navigating across cultural difference informed my efforts to be culturally equitable and inclusive. But how could I expand that to include other forms of diversity? How could I create a learning environment that welcomes and invites diverse perspectives? I was particularly focused on moving away from putting people from the dominant culture/race as the focal norm and considering everyone else as diverse.

The first time I taught the Global and Diverse Families course, I became aware that many learners from the dominant culture did not think they had a culture. As a result, they located themselves in the center, and placed people who were not like them in the "other" category rather than considering themselves as part of the diversity that exists, a tension I identified at the beginning of this chapter. This idea persisted in subsequent classes I taught, and I know that many other intercultural educators have come across it as well.

To address this, I consciously include examples and talk about culture from an inclusive standpoint, raising examples from the White Euro-American culture (my own, it bears mentioning) in addition to highlighting examples of families in other parts of the world. It is my intention to provide examples to which all of my students can relate to encourage them to understand themselves as cultural beings. This also opens possibilities to discuss issues of privilege, how it plays out in intercultural interactions, and how it can be leveraged toward positive outcomes. If our own revision and reflection as faculty are necessary components to the development of an intercultural pedagogy, they are also important threads for learners to be exposed to as they shape their own intercultural approaches.

An in-class interaction illustrates my point. We had finished watching several personal culture digital stories and were discussing themes that ran through the stories and how the themes were similar and different across students. One learner commented on how interesting she found these stories and how glad she was that I had required them to create and share them with classmates. Then she asked, "But how do we know about others in 'real life'?" "Good question," I responded. "How do we begin to engage with others to learn about their cultures?" Very quickly, a learner wearing a hijab spoke up and said, "Well, don't ask me where I'm from!" Admittedly, I wasn't prepared for this!

I responded to her remark by commenting that as a person who is generally interested in peoples' cultures and wants to learn about them, I have been guilty of posing that question to people who look different than me. She smiled and said, "But I can tell that you're interested." I asked her how she could tell; her response was that tone of voice, facial expression, and place made a difference: "Where are *you* from?" asked of a cashier in Walmart by a customer with a defiant attitude is different than the "Where are you from?" question raised in a social setting with a look of interest on the asker's face.

Many learners nodded; they understood the difference that nonverbal behaviors, voice inflection, and context made to the interpretation of the intent behind the question.

Another learner of color picked up the thread and said she'd like to learn more about the cultures of White Euro-Americans. In response, a White Euro-American woman admitted that until this assignment, she didn't think she had a culture and was still struggling to describe it. I seized the moment to interject that the fact that White Euro-Americans asked others where they were from but were never asked that same question in a way that inferred outsider status illustrated the privilege they have in our society.

I decided in that moment that I, too, would be vulnerable and share an important lesson I learned a few years ago at an awards ceremony in my college. My dean, who was giving out the awards, came upon a name that she was not confident she could pronounce. She speculated that it was a Thai name, and knowing that I speak Thai, asked me to come to the front and present the award. I looked at the name, also concluded it was Thai, but was also not confident that I would correctly pronounce it after reading the English spelling. Speaking in Thai, I prefaced my public announcement of her name by asking for forgiveness if I mispronounced it. I got no response from the undergraduate student, but I did get a response, in Thai, from the adult Euro-American woman who was with her at the event. She explained to me, in Thai language, that like me she had lived in Thailand for a period of time and had adopted her daughter, who was raised in the United States and did not speak a word of Thai. We both laughed at this ironic interchange, but it was an important (and embarrassing) lesson for me to learn about assumptions based on appearances and names.

The students in my class laughed at my story, but I think that they appreciated that I shared my mistake with them. At the end of class, many learners stopped to thank me for the discussion we'd had, saying that they appreciated the honest interaction among their peers and my openness to letting the discussion unfold. The following morning I received an e-mail from the learner who had initiated the conversation with her "Please don't ask me where I'm from" comment. She shared a TED Talk by Taiye Selasi titled "Don't Ask Me Where I'm From, Ask Where I'm a Local" (2015). I posted the video on our course site and invited learners to give me their feedback. Their positive responses resulted in my decision to show the TED Talk the following semester and use Selasi's "3Rs: Relationships, Rituals, and Restrictions" to frame the personal culture digital story assignment.

The first time we used this frame in the Global and Diverse Families course, learners of color readily understood and communicated Selasi's idea of restrictions in their reflections; yet by and large, White Euro-American learners struggled to identify their restrictions. Many did not include any in their stories; others who included them mentioned temporary restrictions due to being in school and having neither the time nor money to do everything they desired. This prompted me to spend more time discussing restrictions, both their existence and the lack thereof due to privilege in future terms.

I also realized that U.S.-based learners needed to understand privilege on a global scale. This was emphasized to me when I was pushed to consider privilege through a very insightful reflection by one of my Hmong students who traveled with me to Thailand. When he interacted with Thai Hmong, it struck him how privileged he was as an American Hmong person. Thinking of privilege that way was new to him and he struggled to make sense of it. He commented on how privilege had always been discussed in terms of race and class in his U.S. classrooms but now he had to rethink it in terms of national origin. We talked about Hmong Thais' experiences of discrimination in Thailand and how that might be similar or different from what he'd experienced in America. But he kept coming back to his "relative" privilege as a Hmong American. It was an interesting idea that I had not considered before.

Reflecting on these serendipitous learning moments for both students reminds me of the challenge instructors face when sensitive conversations arise. These are not easy conversations to facilitate. It's often in retrospect when I do the second-guessing about "why didn't I think quickly enough to say x" that the real learning for me takes place. Reflection on these difficult interactions is critical. Thinking about what I might have said differently or better adds new insights and facilitation techniques to my teaching repertoire. I also believe that sharing personal stories of mistakes and how one has grown from them teaches important lessons—willingness to admit to not ever arriving at "competence," the importance of being vulnerable to others—risking that you might not always get it right, but that you are willing to authentically and respectfully engage with others, and humbly accepting that we're all learning.

My ongoing journey is an exemplar of our assertion that we continue to develop our expertise and that the process involves ongoing revision and reflection. Even though I was developing my pedagogy before I became fully aware that this was occurring, I am increasingly conscious of where I want to go and what I need to do to get there. As my intercultural pedagogy develops, I am more reflective, more critical, more proactive, and hopefully more effective as a teacher. For example, I am increasingly reflective about the tone and quality of interactions in class, critically analyzing how I may influence students, positively or negatively. I am more intentional about initiating important conversations, listening to and taking cues from the learners, being open to directions they want to explore, and being aware of interactions among learners, including me, that allow the possibilities for significant learning to occur. There is also more intentionality in my reflections about assignments, considering ways that I can more explicitly describe the intended goals, be increasingly clear in the instructions, and critically evaluate the quality of the artifacts that learners produce.

As mentioned earlier, participating in the university's Internationalizing Teaching and Learning faculty fellowship was a pivotal point in my intercultural pedagogy development. Involvement with wise and experienced mentors and like-minded colleagues in a community of practice facilitated my learning and development in very important ways. It helped me become clear about many aspects of my pedagogy and how I enacted it in my teaching, from naming the paradigm that shapes my understanding of families and culture to recognizing the presence of three interrelated threads that needed to be more effectively woven and articulated to students in the course, to reshaping learning objectives and aligning activities that supported their manifestation in learners.

Meeting New Challenges Over Time

Just as I was thinking that I had reached a point where I had a solid course that (a) aligned with my pedagogical approach; (b) included the learning objectives I felt necessary to teach about families and culture, intercultural interacting, globalization, and social justice; (c) required meaningful learning activities (readings, discussions, in-class experiences, digital personal culture story, digital ethno-narrative, and service-learning); and (d) used assessments that aligned with my pedagogy and effectively evaluated learning, I was told that the class would be offered online the following semester. I struggled to wrap my head around how I could achieve the same level of learning in a virtual environment. And quite honestly, I was upset that my work to reach this stage of course development would have to be revised significantly to be effective as an online course. I was able to convince my department chair to offer the course in a hybrid format rather than fully online, which helped my angst considerably. Nonetheless, this was a major change that required a great deal of work.

I have made conscious decisions about which learning activities can be effectively used in the online learning environment and which need to be taught in the face-to-face sessions. Specifically, activities that are scheduled into in-class sessions are structured around three criteria. First, they foster the development of intercultural sensitivity—a personal frame activity, sharing, analyzing and discussing personal culture digital stories, and concepts of culture and intercultural interacting. Second, they contribute to understanding the complexity and variation of culture and its influence on families through synthesizing themes from the digital ethno-narratives and noting differences and similarities within and across cultures. Third, they are activities that illuminate the values of social justice—a synthesis and discussion of service-learning experiences and discussions that focus on privilege and professional commitment to serving vulnerable families.

This course focuses on family dynamics of various cultural groups across the world in their economic, political, and sociocultural contexts. Learners will examine the interdependence of family, kin, culture, class, community, education, religion, politics, and economics within and across cultures. The course will facilitate the development of intercultural sensitivity, a skill that is increasingly important in today's global environment. Learners will engage in community-based service-learning, small-group online and in-person dialogue, and reflective writing. Learners will develop qualitative research skills through the creation of a digital ethno-narrative and the analysis of peers' work. A final comprehensive synthesis paper will be used to evaluate student learning.

I am committed to continuing to develop my own ability to interact interculturally, keeping a philosophy of cultural humility at the core of my learning. Although I can confidently navigate the Thai culture, I must be cautious about being overly confident as time goes on. For example, I developed much of what I know over a 35-year time span, but contemporary Thais are very different from the Thais of three decades ago, particularly in urban areas. I must be continually observing cues, asking questions, testing hypotheses, and checking out my interpretations with cultural insiders. What stays relatively constant culturally, and what changes with globalization and changes in economy, and so forth? When I encounter a new experience of difference, how can I apply what I've learned from navigating one culture to effectively interacting in a new culture? What is the essence of that navigational process, and what are the tools in my kit that can be transferred and/or applied across spaces of difference?

Conclusion

Any human development journey of value involves phases that are exciting; dull; arduous; rewarding; frustrating; and at times, unconscious. Mine has been no different; I believe I have made significant progress toward developing and enacting an intercultural pedagogy in the learning spaces I create. And I believe that those efforts have resulted in significant learning for students. The tensions outlined at the beginning of this chapter have abated, but they continue to present themselves in new and subtle ways. I know I am more attentive to them and am confident that I have more resources in my toolkit to work through them. Each group of learners is unique—in essence they create a classroom culture that I need to observe, interpret, and navigate each semester. My greatest current challenge is being able to do that when I have very minimal in-person contact with learners. It limits my ability to be responsive to their needs and interests, a key tenet of an intercultural pedagogy. It reduces the joy I receive from engaging with increasingly diverse groups of learners. But my commitment to help learners develop intercultural sensitivity so they can respectfully and effectively support diverse families in their work as family science professionals remains strong. I need to return to my community of practice for support to critically analyze the new tensions and opportunities that online environments present. The "miles," the bends in the road, the potholes, and the breathtaking "aha!" moments on my journey thus far have taught me well. I look forward to what lies ahead.

6

FACILITATING PRODUCTIVE DISCOMFORT IN INTERCULTURAL CLASSROOMS

As we undertake the final revision of this chapter, it is November 2016, just a week after the U.S. presidential election. During the campaign and particularly in the past week, on campuses and around the country, there has been a reported increase in the number of hate crimes and hate speech incidents. Our own students are reporting on troubling interactions they have experienced or witnessed on campus. Campus counseling centers and some academic programs have been actively communicating to students about safe spaces and mental health and have been hosting meetings and spaces dedicated to ensuring a sense of belonging and to healing and community wellness. The current context affirms the urgent need for actively inclusive classrooms and for educators who can invite students to practice and to deepen their intercultural understanding and communication. As educators, we are obligated to ensure that our classrooms are safe spaces for *all* students to learn, to listen, and to contribute.

In "A Talk to Teachers," James Baldwin (1963) told the educators gathered in his audience, "It is your responsibility to change society if you think of yourself as an educated person." Baldwin described education as fundamentally about "the right and the necessity to examine everything." Baldwin speaks to the crux of our task as intercultural pedagogues: we must teach our students how to become critical and reflective examiners. In order to do that, we must conduct such examinations ourselves; we must examine our values and how they do or do not manifest in our teaching; we must examine whether our classrooms support inclusivity, and whether our teaching is supporting not only disciplinary learning, skills, and habits of mind but also those habits and skills that support intercultural understanding and respect.

In order to do that work, as we argued in Part One of this book, we must be committed to and prepared for discussions that engage tense and ambiguous issues and feelings. Further, we need tools to guide students in generative interactions with one another and with multiple perspectives and identities presented by course content and assignments. However, many of us feel under- or ill-equipped to design or facilitate these kinds of interactions. As we established in Part One, most of us were never given any systematic preparation for intercultural teaching. In fact, many of us receive little to no education in *teaching* as teacher education in general remains undervalued in and by higher education.

Throughout the book, we argue that it is not enough to conduct a critical examination or to espouse an intercultural pedagogy. It is essential that we also *model* intercultural learning and reflection for students within our classrooms and instill in them a desire to do this work. In that spirit, we explicitly provide models for our readers. The book is grounded in two case studies, beginning with Bob's and Catherine's personal reflections and extending to their case studies, wherein we were invited into their processes of examining their own intercultural development and intentionally seeking to develop and practice intercultural pedagogy. Now, in this final chapter, we want to focus on student interactions in our classrooms—with one another and with course content—and provide some coaching about how intercultural pedagogy can shape the ways we design, structure, facilitate, and follow up on interactions.

First, we will flesh out the importance of productive discomfort in the intercultural classroom—what is productive discomfort and why is it important to this work? We then move into a discussion of the characteristics that shape the design and implementation/facilitation of effective interactions in the intercultural classroom. We will end by providing and reflecting on examples of interactions in our courses that were uncomfortable and generated discomfort, but perhaps did not transpire productively or yield productive outcomes. For each example, we will apply hindsight in order to consider how we have redesigned the interaction or how we approach or facilitate it differently in light of the experience. Facilitating productive discomfort through interactions requires not only our students but also us as teachers to continually reflect on what supports inclusion and on how we can refine and hone our pedagogy so as to continue to contribute to the development of intercultural skills.

Productive Discomfort

> If the wariness about discomfort is stronger than the desire to hear different viewpoints because engaging difference is uncomfortable, then the quest for diversity is hollow no matter what the demographic statistics on a campus reflect. (Liebowitz, 2007)

As we have consistently emphasized in this book, intercultural learning is not "comfortable." It is characterized by various tensions, it requires dissonance, and ambiguity is inevitable. Many of these are antithetical to how we and many of our students may have learned to think about learning. Productive discomfort is essential for all participants in an intercultural classroom, students and teacher alike. So becoming familiar with it, accepting it, and pursuing it—as well as being able to discern productive discomfort from unproductive discomfort—is important.

The value of discomfort is one of the tenets of transformational learning; we highlighted this when we spoke of its value in self-reflection and how that value transfers to the learning environment. Mezirow (1997) argues that we all operate from what he calls a "frame of reference," which encompasses cognitive, conative, and emotional components composed of two dimensions: habits of mind and point of view. This frame of reference signifies a comfort zone within which we can operate with little resistance, particularly as it is reinforced through experiences, memories, and interactions with others. It requires a higher-order type of thinking to examine our own preconceived notions or to encounter different perspectives and to accept, integrate, and find space for those perspectives in our own frames of reference. It is here that the realities of the intercultural classroom become apparent and may cause difficulties as individuals with differing viewpoints come together in the learning environment.

In her scholarship on the pedagogy of discomfort Boler (1999) examines the impact of binary attitudes on the learning environment. When one side of the binary is viewed as *us, good, right,* and *moral,* and the other side of the binary (*them*) is viewed as *undesirable* (either *bad, evil,* or *wrong*), Boler (1999) suggests that learners intentionally establish emotional distance between themselves and those with differing viewpoints, affiliations, or identities. The lack of connection may serve a variety of functions depending on who has created that distance; the intentional isolation can perpetuate the beliefs of the status quo (e.g., "Why should I have to adjust my behavior beyond majority norms?") or may also be used as a survival strategy for those who are coping with social injustice (e.g., "I can be understood only by people who share my own background and identity."). Both signify a retreat to Mezirow's (1997) "comfort zone," where the exchange of ideas feels less taxing and more familiar.

Other potential byproducts of binary attitudes are student disengagement, conflict, hostility, and resistance—enacted visibly or subtly toward peers and instructors. In 1999, Boler asserted that matters of diversity (e.g., race, language, age, gender, culture, socioeconomic status) were particularly susceptible to binary attitudes and binary language that make ongoing conversation and learning particularly challenging. Recent reports across our campuses and in the media underscore for us that these assertions remain true and that binary attitudes and language that characterized the 2016 election cycle have carried grave impacts on all levels of education and within social structures across the United States and the globe.

Facilitating Interactions

We place significant focus in this volume on the integration of tensions and dissonance, largely in the context of our personal and pedagogical identities, course design, and within the field of higher education. Here, we revisit pedagogy as "the transformation of consciousness that takes place in the intersection of three agencies—the teacher, the learner, and the knowledge they together produce" (Lusted, 1986, p. 3) and focus on two types of interactions that are essential to the intercultural classroom: those that occur among students in the learning environment and those that take place between a student and the ideas or perspectives raised in course content or assignments. We focus on interactions because they serve as the core of the intercultural classroom, and yet they do not necessarily come "naturally" to teachers or students nor are they always comfortable or complete.

Inclusive classroom interactions must be characterized by respect for one another and for different ideas; an intercultural classroom must actively invite and productively engage multiple perspectives and ways of seeing. This can seem like a mammoth and complex charge, given the complexity of the "live" class environment (whether your course is online or in a classroom) and the challenge of effectively honoring and integrating various identities, worldviews, and life experiences in the learning environment. The intercultural pedagogical task is, therefore, largely rooted in how to create the conditions for students to engage with each other and with ideas in ways that prompt learning and to simultaneously develop the facilitation skills to further those interactions.

Classroom climate is a powerful, ever-present element of the "live" classroom and a critical tool in intercultural pedagogy. Regardless of whether you acknowledge it or intentionally develop it, a classroom climate is established in every classroom and it is not static. Climate is a way of naming the factors that determine whether participants perceive that their contributions and their presence are not only welcome but also vital to the learning enterprise. Climate is a concept that helps us attend to the quality of the learning environment that we are cocreating with our students, and to the types of interactions we are facilitating among students and between student and course content.

The most successful teaching and facilitation attempts take place on a solid foundation of positive classroom environment and rapport (Lee, Williams, Shaw, & Jie, 2014). There are many ways in which relationship building can occur, enabling course-related change to happen. Some of the strategies that we use are very simple and others are more complex; as always with human interaction, there are risks involved that relate to self-disclosure and sharing, both on the part of the students and on the part of the instructor. What follows is a practical list of those strategies that can be used in nearly every learning environment:

1. Learn student names and continually attempt correct pronunciation. Encourage this behavior for all members of the class.
2. Do not assume that all students come from a learning tradition of class-based discussion; if possible, try to understand the level of familiarity your students have with peer learning and classroom interaction.
3. Provide a structure for students to reflect on what supports a feeling of being respected and being able to learn; this may be an online activity or can be done with notecards (anonymously) in the classroom.
4. Clearly articulate the value of learning through interaction and among peers.
5. As a class, collectively discuss and establish a set of classroom guidelines to ensure a respectful environment; identify and codify expectations collectively and explicitly.
6. Integrate frequent opportunities for low-stakes discussion and sharing of differing opinions.
7. Provide time for quiet writing and organization of thoughts before open class discussion begins.
8. Assign ungraded postdiscussion reflection assignments to process the group discussion and to provide feedback to the facilitator regarding the discussion experience.
9. Be willing to revisit topics after class with individual students and with your class as a whole if you think that further discussion will be of benefit.
10. Share aspects of your own culture and life experiences with your students, especially if you are asking them to do the same among themselves.

As with other teaching activities, these rapport-building strategies require intentional alignment between your teaching style, your student audience, and the objectives that you are trying to achieve. They may also take some practice and discomfort of your own as you experiment with ways to integrate these into your teaching. Adopting one of these strategies alone does not constitute an intercultural pedagogical approach, but openness to reflect on your classroom climate and effort to improve it for all students do model an intercultural pedagogical approach.

Our underlying assumption, established in chapter 2 and revisited throughout this book, is that the pedagogical quality of these interactions is based in large part on an instructor's intentional learning design and facilitation. It is not enough to simply have interactions among individuals; it is essential that the interactions be purposeful, scaffolded, and relevant to the goals at hand. Although tensions and dissonance are natural in the learning process and in the intercultural development process, interactions require intention, awareness, and facilitation to ensure that all participants can productively engage these tensions. As with the inclusion strategies, facilitation also demands practice, revision, and refinement. In that spirit, we offer the following examples as models of this process. Building upon Bob's and Catherine's personal and professional reflections and their detailed accounts of "interculturalizing" their courses, these next accounts recount actual interactions in Bob's and Catherine's classes and the decisions they made around facilitating difficult conversations and learning situations.

In selecting these examples, we wanted to represent a breadth of encounters—ones that happen in person, online, among peers, and with information and ideas. In each of the four cases, the author sets the scene, describes the intended learning, and then details what actually happened, regardless of the intended design. In each, there is reflection and revision, albeit—and authentically—in different order depending on the situations that Bob and Catherine describe. It is our hope that these narratives show, rather than tell or direct, ways that the themes of this book enter into the "live classroom" and our encounters with students.

Catherine: A Challenge

Facilitating Exploration of Values, Perceptions, and Judgments With Students

Global and Diverse Families—*undergraduate course, University of Minnesota–Twin Cities*

Background

In my course Global and Diverse Families, I require students to engage in 22 hours of service-learning. After learners have volunteered for about half of the hours required, they share their experiences with each other in small groups in a face-to-face session. I ask them to describe the organization or agency, their position, and what they do when they volunteer. Then they share at least one aspect of their experience that excites them and one aspect that challenges them. As students talk, I walk around the room and listen to snippets of the conversations. The "flavor" of these is typically positive, with threads of similar experiences across learners and across organizations. Occasionally, however, I encounter a learner's report for which I feel I need to intervene, most often due to hearing negative comments about "them," meaning those who are served at the site where students volunteer.

The Interaction

In one specific encounter, a learner described his volunteer site to his peers as "chaotic" and "out of control"; he said that the children were undisciplined and disrespectful. He then went on to explain how uncomfortable he was as a volunteer; his experience was not good because of this chaos. I stopped and listened for a while to see if others would ask him questions to get at the "why" for the chaos he described. When that didn't occur, I decided to join the conversation. I asked him to think about the organization. What was their mission? Who did they serve? How old were the children? What time of the day did he volunteer and what were the children doing before he arrived? I asked him to describe the staffing for the program. What was the child-staff ratio? How were they reacting to the "chaos" or to "undisciplined" children?

We spent some time talking about children's developmental stages, the nature of nonprofit work and the challenges of funding and staffing, and the overall mission of providing supervised space for children. I then asked him (and others who had agreed that what he described was "chaotic") to stop for a minute and hold up the mirror to see themselves and their experiences as part of the equation in the volunteer site. What were they bringing from their own early experiences of programs like preschool, after-school care, and their home lives? What were the rules and expectations of "proper" conduct? How and from whom did they learn about those rules?

Then, because I teach a family course, I asked the students to reflect on the lives of the families reflected in these children. What might be happening at home that these children bring into the program environment? Might their parents be struggling to make ends meet? Were they working several jobs and perhaps not at home to monitor and model as much as these college students' parents had been during their formative years? How might parenting be different for these children than what they experienced? Were there cultural differences playing out in behaviors? I encouraged learners to use the human ecological model to stay in an observe/describe mode, to consider the family, the human-built environment, and the sociocultural environment to try to understand the situations before labeling, evaluating, or judging.

I also encouraged them to reflect on their own socialization and how they learned "appropriate" behavior based on their particular family and sociocultural environments. Finally, I asked the young man who had described his volunteer experience to think about how he might insert some "order" into what he considered a chaotic experience. Could he prepare some developmentally appropriate, large-group games that would engage the children in activities that involved large-motor skills and burned off some of their energy?

Reflection

I believe that the result of this question/reflection exercise was that the learners in that particular group developed a more complex understanding of the situation described by their peer. Although the situation was presented by one person, several others had similar reactions to their sites, especially if they involved children. But I could sense that all learners around the table were reflecting on their own experiences, regardless of where they were volunteering. How might they have been using their own experiences to interpret another's behavior? Why would it be helpful to "hold up the mirror" to reflect on how "I" was socialized before making assumptions about another? And for this class on global and diverse families, how does parenting differ across culture, worldviews, value systems, life experiences, and/or social location?

In hindsight, I spent about 20 minutes spontaneously unpacking this conversation with one group and not with the others. I was sorry that others hadn't heard the interaction because I expect that similar negative conversations had happened around the room. In retrospect, I realized my questions were too simplistic. I was expecting a deep, reflective response from a surface-level question: What excites or challenges you in your service-learning experience? I also realized that getting to deeper levels of reflection about their service-learning experiences requires facilitation, asking questions, following up, and gently challenging assumptions.

Revision

As a result of what I learned from this particular interaction, I now use a fishbowl format for in-class service-learning reflections. I create groups of learners with similar service-learning experiences. One might be composed of those who volunteer in after-school group programs, another in individual tutoring programs, and another in domestic violence shelters and/or prevention programs. One of the groups sits in an inner circle; the remaining learners sit in an outside circle and observe the process. I pose questions and facilitate the conversation with inner-circle group members, moving the conversation from observation and description to self-reflection and insight. This format allows me to have an in-depth conversation and process with the focal group and extend the learning to the learners who observe.

Postreflection on Pedagogy

The graduate teaching assistant who had listened to my interaction with the group that day asked how I'd learned when to intervene and how to facilitate these types of conversations. She said that she felt ill-prepared to do this in real time in a classroom setting. I remember telling her that this was something I'd developed over time and with practice. The first time I created some "productive discomfort" by challenging someone in a classroom, I felt like I'd really messed up. I "relived" the process over and over with whichever colleague happened to be in my path, trying to come to some peace that I'd handled it in a responsible and "correct" manner. To this day, I continue to have those same feelings. Honestly, it's so much easier to pretend to be oblivious and avoid these conversations. But a reflexive teacher realizes that each situation will present itself with new challenges, depending on the learners involved and the topic at hand. Some of the most important learning happens through these types of impromptu interactions, albeit if they are handled well. But an instructor can tip the scales in a positive direction if there is an established respectful learning environment that normalizes interactions that involve asking questions of others to seek better understanding of differing perspectives and of reflecting to seek better understanding of one's own perspective. It's also important to move conversations fairly quickly from an interaction with only one learner to one that involves all learners in critical thinking and self-reflection. In my example earlier, I knew that others in the group had experienced similar things in their service-learning sites and were nonverbally agreeing with his evaluation of the situation. So after an initial acknowledgment of what I'd just heard, I quickly moved the conversation to a group level and invited all into the process. The ability to self-reflect and be aware of what has influenced how we perceive and experience the world is critical to effective intercultural interaction.

Bob: The Bridge

Facilitating and Using Difficult Experiences in the Classroom

Educational Movements Past and Present: Multicultural Perspectives—
undergraduate course, University of Minnesota–Twin Cities

Background

The word *racism* elicits discomfort for many reasons. Some students worry
that it will be used to further separate persons, point fingers of guilt, or
produce predictable teacher monologues that lead to no useful purposes.
Moreover, challenging words and ideas like *racism* are skipped over because
of false notions that such words hold commonly understood meanings. As
a result, students avoid the word or cling to old superficial meanings that
buffer engagement with new, uncomfortable, and disruptive viewpoints.
As the teacher of a new course, Educational Movements Past and Present:
Multicultural Perspectives, I decided to invest significant classroom time in
exploring the meaning of *racism* and its impact on educational structures,
opportunities, and exclusions in the United States.

We began our exploration as a class with dictionaries, which we soon
found muddied rather than clarified definitions and conceptions of *racism*.
I then asked students to look online for definitions. While walking around
the classroom to observe groups of 5 to 8 students at round tables earnestly
seeking definitions of *racism* on their cell phones and comparing what
they were finding with each other, I saw many furrowed brows. As we
debriefed small-group findings as a full class, students observed that definitions of *racism* were very similar to definitions of *prejudice*. Were there
differences in word meanings or did *prejudice* and *racism* actually mean the
same thing?

I found that, despite our review of scholarly literature differentiating
racism and prejudice, students were still conflating the words within writing assignments and classroom discussions. To them, racism and prejudice
remained the same. Important distinctions between the words were lost or
forgotten and the important work of scholars, such as Beverly Tatum and
Derald Wing Sue, integral to the course, was largely set aside. I desperately
wanted students to understand how *power* and *systems* that perpetuated power
were integral parts of racism. I wanted them to know that not everyone had
historically conferred power or access to systems of power. Scholarship and
facilitated classroom searches for definitions were not providing such understandings among my diverse students. I needed something more—some connection that would make the meaning of *racism* clearer, more relevant, and
perhaps more personal. While searching for a pedagogical way to do so, an

event on our campus provided an unanticipated opportunity and a sudden but very necessary revision to my pedagogical approach.

The Interaction

The lengthy Washington Avenue Bridge spans the Mississippi River on our campus, enabling persons to walk between the east and west portions of the Minneapolis campus. An enclosed center portion of the bridge used for covered pedestrian traffic features wall panels that are assigned to university-registered groups. These groups—mostly student groups—can paint their assigned panels to advertise and promote their respective organizations. During the 2016 presidential election, the College Republicans painted one of their panels with the Trump-Pence campaign slogan, "Build the Wall."

Sometime thereafter, the panel with the slogan and the adjoining panel with the names Trump and Pence had spray-painted over them the words, "Stop White Supremacy." This ignited a very public debate about racism, First Amendment rights, campus climate, and other related dynamics on our campus. Further, a written response by the university's president was widely perceived as defending the rights of those expressing "hate speech" rather than expressing empathy and support for members of the community who felt targeted by the "Build the Wall" slogan, feared for their safety, and felt disenfranchised by the university. Some students e-mailed me about the "paint the bridge incident" as it came to be known, asking for my interpretation of it and expressing fear for their personal safety in the aftermath. I decided then and there to abandon my plans for the next class session (which would occur just a few hours later) and, instead, to facilitate a discussion about "paint the bridge."

Revision

During class, I projected a photo of the bridge panels with the original and spray-painted messages and briefly but sincerely acknowledged the pain and division they caused on campus. Left aside were my prior-planned slides further exploring the meaning of racism. I opened the class session by sharing that I cared deeply about the well-being of each student, that I valued them, and that I was available to anyone who wanted to talk about the bridge individually and privately. I also shared that some members of our community felt unwanted, unsafe, and unvalued given all that had occurred. I asked students about how they felt and what questions the "paint the bridge" incident raised for them and how we might respond individually or collectively. At my invitation students reflected individually and wrote notes about their feelings and questions. I then asked that discussions commence between two or three students, then tables of eight, and then the full class.

Students spent nearly two hours actively sharing and discussing their views and relating it to course content—including the meaning of racism. I was deeply touched by how students interacted with one another with sincere compassion and care and was delighted by the elegant connections that they made between the meaning of racism and the bridge. It took a recent event, in close proximity to their lives, and involving people whom they cared about (fellow students) to connect a word—*racism*—to its deeper meanings, including real notions about power, distributions of power, and systems of power on our campus. What students could not derive from quoted scholarship on PowerPoint slides or handouts they could derive from lived experience and interactions with other students.

Reflection

This did not come about easily, neatly, or predictably. I was nervous about how the class session would unfold. For example, I observed one exchange between two students—one White and the other of personally disclosed Mexican ancestry—who passionately but respectfully discussed the necessity of upholding freedom of expression while counterbalancing such rights with the protection of students who experience some such speech as expressions of hate and the incitement of violence. They communicated very different perspectives—including notions of the power of historically conferred White privilege and supremacy—and shared differing lived experiences. But both heard each other and made connections to course concepts—including racism—in ways that my original pedagogical plans would never achieve. The White student later reflected in her final paper for the course:

> I get to interact with people who are not like me and also see their point of view on a certain subject or topic which is crucial to learning more about that subject/topic because I would never have thought about it in that sort of way. Also students learn how something actually might be affecting another student in your class, but it doesn't affect you so you don't worry about it. The whole Build the Wall scandal that happened on the bridge at our university is an example. I didn't really think that much when the painting was written, but going to CI 1121 and actually talking about it with students who were affected by it made me have a whole different perspective on the situation. I got to learn where they were coming from and how their concern for their safety can affect me because I would never want my classmates to feel unsafe like that, nor would I ever want to feel that way as well. With that whole situation it really opened my eyes and so, I am a poster child for why schools need to have diversity within it because a student, like me, can gain so much from just one different perspective.

I do not believe that this reflection and insight would have emerged from a personally detached academic conversation about the meaning of racism between me and students. Rather, it required a sudden revision in my pedagogical plan as enabled by a campus event to bring diverse students into active conversation about power, systems of power, and the ongoing relevancy of racism. The discussion made the word *racism* come alive in a productive way that enabled understanding and growth. As a class, we followed up on this discussion throughout the remainder of the course when we examined different forms of privilege, power, systems of oppression, and examples of disruptions of power in educational history. It breathed personal experience and connection into the course in a new way and invited similar personal connections and relevancy as we proceeded through the semester. It was challenging and uncomfortable for me to depart from a planned class session. However, the value of doing so was apparent in the meaning-making that the students produced from the discomforting occurrence of a race-based event on campus. This was a reminder of how productive discomfort can emerge within a classroom when we are willing to sometimes abandon our plans, openly acknowledge the pain and fear that many students experience, and trust that students will engage, empathize, and learn from their peers within the context of a very disquieting event.

Catherine: The Forum

Facilitating Challenging Discussions Online

Global and Diverse Families—*undergraduate course, University of Minnesota–Twin Cities*

Background

A new challenge arose for me when my course was changed from a face-to-face to a hybrid format, meaning that much of the student interaction moved into the online realm. I mourned the loss of real-time interaction with my students and felt that their learning would be diminished. I struggled to revise the course to accommodate the new format, scheduling content-focused learning during online weeks of the semester, and intercultural interaction-learning during face-to-face sessions. My rationale was that the latter needed more instructor facilitation and real-time discussion to support the development of learners' abilities to interact across cultural boundaries. Yet one particular interaction online provided a vivid reminder of how content and process are inexplicably intertwined. The following is an example of how a seemingly "objective" discussion of a textbook idea resulted in a valuable lesson in intercultural interacting.

The Interaction

Most instructors use online threaded discussions to foster understanding of key concepts from what learners are reading or viewing. This particular discussion asked learners to discuss an idea from their textbook related to globalization and families: Are you a skeptic, a hyperglobalist, or a transformationalist regarding the impact of cultural globalization and families? Identify which stance resonates the most with you, and discuss why you think this way. What aspect of family life might be most vulnerable to changes due to globalization?

A learner who identified as a Somali-born Muslim woman wrote the following:

H: *I am a transformationalist because I believe in globalization being ever so changing. Also I believe globalization brings different cultures together. Which is beneficial because this will bring new ideas and perspectives. This benefits society in many ways. It encourages diversity and makes people more open-minded to new cultures and ideas. It also helps to eliminate racism.*

One aspect that has brought negative affect to my family since migrating to the U.S. was keeping our culture alive. I am Muslim and I was born in Somalia. I lived in the U.S. my whole life. Since I was 5 years old, but my parents struggled with keeping me and my siblings to act on our culture, religion, and language. My parents wanted me and my siblings to have a normal American childhood, but they did not want us to forget our culture and religion. Thanks to my parents, I can speak fluent Somali and I know everything there is to my culture and religion. In addition, I can speak fluent English and I know how the American way of life works. All in all, I think the downside of globalization is losing your culture. But other than that, globalization is great for society. You just have to find that balance.

This spurred a response from a learner who shared in her personal cultural story earlier in the semester that she identified as a White, middle-class female and an active-duty Army reservist:

A: *I am interested in the reasons you say that you are a transformationalist. None of the three understandings of globalization believe it is bad or good phenomenon as you allude; rather they look at the impact/presence of globalization. Skepticists don't dislike globalization nor do they disagree that there are benefits to globalization; they simply don't believe that it has as big of an impact on our everyday life as a transformationalist does. I would challenge you to go back and look at the true definitions of the words as the author presents in our textbook and really reflect on why you adhere to transformationalism.*

A different group member affirmed H's post:

J: *I think that what you said about finding balance is really important. It must be really hard moving to a new society and trying to hold on to your old culture and yet trying to fit in, in a new place. If you assimilate too much you lose your culture and your connection to your heritage but yet if you don't assimilate enough you end up an outsider. I think for each family it is important for them to find a balance that works best for them. It sounds like you and your family found a balance that works really well for you.*

H: *I agree, J! My parents did not want me and my siblings to be an outsider. Which is why they encouraged us to learn English and adapt to the U.S. way of life. But then again they did not want us to lose our culture.*

A learner who identified as an African-born immigrant woman in her personal culture story added her support for H's response and challenged A about the way she responded:

S: *". . . global transformationalists contend that cultural transmission is complex, nuanced, and sometimes contradictory." (Karraker, p. 99).*

I didn't see anywhere in this post where it says that globalization is just good or just bad. I noticed that H pulled out positive and negative aspects and proved why cultural transmission is complex. She points out the nuance of transmission and assimilation, and seeing as that's a way of thinking that global transformationalists tend to take, I totally get why she would choose it. I challenge you to respond to the actual post of your peers and do it in a way that is a bit more respectful.

Learners in this exchange not only were discussing ideas but also had added a layer of complexity to the interactions by discussing the tone and intent of the communication:

H: *My explanation for choosing transformationalist was based off of both negative and positive perspectives. I mention both perspectives in my post. You should look back at my post if you're confused. P.S. don't question my knowledge, that is disrespectful! If you have future questions regarding my post, try asking in a respectful manner. We are not in high school. No need to ask in a disrespectful manner.*

H: *P.S. A, if you don't have anything positive to say, "I challenge you" to not make a comment.*

It was time for me to intervene. I struggled to think how I could mediate this interaction, affirm perspectives, and use the situation as a learning opportunity. In real time and space, I'd done this before and believe I was able to model respectful communication when learners share different, and at times, oppositional perspectives. However, doing this *online* posed a new challenge. I immediately speculated that perhaps an underlying context of the interaction stemmed from the fact that the three learners for whom this interaction was uncomfortable brought very different life experiences and cultures to the exchange. Two were recent immigrants from Africa—I imagined that their refugee experiences had deeply shaped their understanding of globalization and heightened their sensitivity to its positive and negative aspects. One learner was from the dominant U.S. culture and was in the military; I imagined how she could be quite oblivious to the experiences of immigrant families. Moreover, American or military cultures might foster a communication style in which challenging was viewed as respectful. Was this miscommunication due to a lack of understanding of another's experience? Was it a result of a clash between high- (African) and low- (military) context cultures? Was A's response, in fact, a microaggression? I had very little on which to base my interpretation. Moreover, the online medium made it difficult to get information that would have helped me understand. So, I decided to respond by writing the following:

Hello group. It seems like we have a bit of tension running through this threaded discussion. I'd like to share my perspective in the spirit of us learning from what happened and striving to improve how things move forward.

A, although I respect that you were trying to initiate a dialogue with H, the last sentence in your response could easily be interpreted as a put-down, basically telling H that she was wrong and that she needed to defend her answer. I would also feel disrespected if I were the one receiving that message, perhaps something you didn't intend.

Online conversations are challenging, so let me offer another way you might have responded that would open up the dialogue between two peers who might disagree with the interpretation, but each has the right to their own interpretation.

Possible response from A: "I wonder, H, if you are interpreting these three globalization perspectives differently than I do. I shared my understanding. Would you please help me understand how you interpreted them and how your interpretation influenced your response? It seems like your personal experience influenced how you interpreted these three understandings—that's really interesting and I'd like to know more."

Possible response from H: "I understand that you might disagree with my answers because your interpretation might be different than mine. But I was offended by the way you 'challenged' me—a word that doesn't invite a respectful dialogue, suggested that your interpretation is the only valid one, and raised intense feelings. Can you help me understand why you felt you had to 'challenge' me to rethink my response?"

I'd like to know how each of you in this group is feeling right now. A, can you see how your frame might have been upsetting? H, can you see how A might have been good in her intentions but her choice of words was the issue? Can you also see

how your response may have escalated the problem? Others, what are you think-
ing? All—can we get back on track and promise to enter into respectful dialogue?
This type of interaction is a good example of how intercultural interacting can be
challenging, made even more so by the online environment when we haven't had
much time to develop personal relationships. Let me hear what you're thinking . . .

My posting elicited the following responses from "A":

A: *I am sorry that you saw my post as negative. I meant "challenge" as in let's*
dig more into our different viewpoints and see why they exist; not as in you are
wrong. I will be sure to rephrase my words more carefully in the future.

A: *You are right, S, my comment came off a little disrespectful. I did not*
intend it in this way. I will double read my responses next time.

In addition, an off-line exchange via e-mail took place:

S: *I thought A had a really strange reaction. I don't think she shared her*
understanding at all. She talked about H "alluding" to globalization being bad
and good but didn't direct us to any places in the post where she felt that vibe.
Plus, H integrated her personal story, which can be pretty vulnerable. In my yeses,
it's intention versus impact. A's intention may have been good but I felt a negative
impact. I don't necessarily think H had the best response, but I understand where
she is coming from. I'd like to participate in a group where it feels like a safe space.
To be honest, my natural reaction after seeing A's response was this doesn't make
sense. Is she racist?

Based on that, I sent the following reply to S:

Thanks for sharing your thoughts, S. You're right that sharing a personal
story can render one vulnerable. I too understand H's response. The two of them
have been in e-mail "conversation" and I think have come to a respectful under-
standing of what happened. A explained her intent and apologized. H accepted.
Hopefully we all learned from the process. I do hope you will be able to spend
time in your group during class next week to visit and rebuild some of the trust
that was eroded. I will make a point to join you so we can work back to a place of
safety, openness, and honesty. Thanks for letting me know how you feel.

And the e-mail chain concluded with the following interaction from A
and H:

A: *Hey H, we have had a few miscommunications in our group discussions*
and I just want to clear the air. It is clear that we view things different, which I
think it very fascinating. I love to discuss differences and why they exist. I apolo-
gize if my "challenge" from last week came off as rude or disrespectful. I meant it
as "let's dig into why our differences exist," not as in you are wrong. I was hoping
we could discuss your take on the text. I will be sure to rephrase my words more
carefully and clearly in the future. Please accept my apology and let's start off on
a better note moving forward.

H: *A, apology accepted. I'm also sorry for overreacting.*

H: *Thanks Dr. Solheim! And I did feel offended but I realized I did over-react. Thank you for addressing the issue that was in hand. I appreciate your help!*

Reflection

This group moved on from this interaction and respectfully engaged with each other for the remainder of the semester. Although it appeared that the final outcome was positive, I continued to ponder my interpretation of the situation and my response. I had focused on responses that would have made the interaction more respectful. However, I didn't unpack the underlying subcontexts that contributed to the misunderstanding. In retrospect, I would have asked more questions to get to the "why" for each learner. Then I might have been able to more effectively help the learners understand how their own and another's perspectives contributed to the interchange. I might have been able to evaluate whether the "challenge" was a micro-aggression. I was also reminded that an online asynchronous learning environment presents challenges to these types of interactions—namely, the inability to wrestle with and resolve issues in real time and in depth.

Revision

Monitoring the interactions of 75 learners in 9 groups over a week's time frame is challenging; the time investment is significant, particularly due to the inconsistent timing of learners' online presence. This makes it difficult to "catch" an unhealthy or unproductive interaction in real time. My experience is that most learners respectfully engage with each other in discussions. However, in this case, if I'd missed the interaction and had not intervened, it would have created an unwelcome environment for several of the learners and it would have allowed another learner to continue in her obliviousness to how her communication style impacted others.

Although this experience reinforced my commitment to regular online engagement with the class, it also spurred me to add this statement to all of my online discussion assignments:

As you engage with others in this discussion thread, keep in mind that you will find that peers understand the material differently and differ in their values, beliefs, and opinions about the topic. This is a good thing! We learn from our differences. However, something you read may feel uncomfortable or even offensive to you. If this happens, please take a step back and ask yourself why you are feeling this way. Then ask yourself how you can respond in a way that leads to better understanding. You might write something like this: "I read your response and don't really understand why you stated x, y, or z. Would you please say more to clarify your response or perspective?" Or, "I was confused by your response. My experiences are very different than yours." Then go on to explain your perspective. If the exchange continues to be uncomfortable or you don't feel as if a direct response is safe, please send your group facilitator or Dr. Solheim an e-mail so that someone can intervene.

Teaching and learning in an online environment add new layers of complexity to teaching intercultural humility. It challenged me to reimagine peer-peer and peer-instructor interactions. It behooved me to be explicit about the "culture of interaction" I expect. And it required that I develop ways to communicate in text what I would communicate verbally and model in a face-to-face class.

Bob: Power and Place

Facilitating Interaction Between Students and Ideas

Educational Movements Past and Present: Multicultural Perspectives— *undergraduate course, University of Minnesota–Twin Cities*

Background

In teaching my new course on educational movements of the past and present from multicultural perspectives, I experienced a healthy pedagogical tension within the course title. The words "educational movements" imply Western-based notions of organization and structure that are often foreign to and exclusive of non-Western peoples, including people who originally inhabited and remain on American landscapes. In such ways, "educational movements" do not adequately represent multicultural perspectives organizationally, epistemologically, spiritually, or pedagogically.

The Interaction

This conceptual tension provided a rich learning and teaching opportunity as I could share contrasts between Western and non-Western ways of knowing and of teaching and learning with students. It also produced much confusion for students given that non-Western scholars often used familiar words like "power" and "place" but the meanings of such words are quite different within non-Western contexts. My students had understandable ongoing difficulty in discerning and relating to the non-Western meanings, as I soon discovered within their writing and my individual meetings with them.

Structurally, I designed my new course to explore foundational differences between Western and non-Western forms of learning, teaching, and knowing. I wanted students to know explicitly that teaching and learning occurred in what is now the United States long before European colonization. It was crucial to me that they engaged with these ideas in their full complexity and that they emerged from the course with an appreciation of the intellectual and spiritual diversity and strength of indigenous peoples. These strengths are too often ignored within textbooks and deny multicultural students the ability to see the diverse ways in which intelligence, teaching, and learning are expressed—including their own.

To partly express the nature of such teaching and learning, I assigned carefully selected reading from indigenous scholars and particularly from Vine Deloria and Daniel Wildcat. Deloria and Wildcat's (2001) book, *Power and Place: Indian Education in America*, expresses foundational differences in the ways in which indigenous peoples experience and communicate learning as part of interaction and spiritual communion with each other, other living beings, and the earth itself. Learning and teaching within indigenous communities value and prioritize lived experience, self-awareness, and the connectivity of all things. "Place" is important given that it produces intimacy with the environment and the ability to learn from it through deep, continuous contact. A place is an experiential teacher. It enables the union of teacher, learner, and self-identity. "Power" is conceived within indigenous cultures as spiritual in nature—the "living energy" that is within the universe which binds us together. Power is relational rather than confrontational (Deloria & Wildcat, 2001, pp. 22–23).

When I assigned a brief writing assignment on power and place within indigenous cultures, I thought the meanings would be clearly distinct from Western notions. Instead, students reverted to Western meanings of power and spoke about conflicts with White settlers in the West or about the use of power against indigenous children within "American Indian" boarding schools. Further, in my individual meetings with students during office hours, I often asked how they interpreted power within the context of indigenous cultures. Again, most often I found students individually reverting to Western definitions and uses of *power* rather than those articulated by Deloria and Wildcat and other indigenous scholars.

Reflection

Clearly, the epistemological differences that shaped differing expressions of teaching and learning between cultures were being lost. Pedagogically, I did not realize how big a challenge these different word meanings would be for students when the course began. Part of my mistake was relying primarily on written communication to express the meanings and differences. That is, I relied almost entirely on Deloria and Wildcat to explain the meanings. Although their writing is exceptionally valuable in understanding the words—and indigenous forms of knowing, teaching, and learning in general—multicultural students still struggle with the meanings and infuse them with Western conceptions. This is particularly so with the word *power*.

Revision

Clearly I needed to revise my approach and help came from a wonderful source. My undergraduate teaching assistant is an accomplished photographer who over the last year influenced me to think more about the use of visuals in my teaching. She is also majoring in elementary education and has exposure to differing pedagogical techniques. As we thought about other visuals we used in class to describe complex ideas, like social constructions of meaning and "personhood," it occurred to us that perhaps the same could be done in helping students to better understand "power" and "place." I turned to Native American art and the interpretation of such art by indigenous scholars. I soon discovered extensive art collections expressing power and place in the form of indigenous American mandalas—circular forms of artistic expression that often explicitly show the interrelationship and energy of living things within a unifying universe. I selected and printed a few examples of such mandalas for use in student meetings and also for visual projection in class. Further, I found strong contrasting examples of Western notions of power in paintings, such as *American Progress* by John Gast in 1872, which portray power in the form of geographic, technological, spiritual, and human domination as White communities rapidly moved westward in the United States under the guise of "manifest destiny."

The inclusion of differing artistic expressions of power and place worked well. Students could better understand the different meanings of the words by linking print and visual sources together rather than relying on print scholarship alone. As I met individually with students, we actively used the visuals, and their verbal and written interpretations of power and place improved dramatically. In reflecting on the difference these visuals made to complex conceptual and interpretive understandings, I remembered that students had told me repeatedly in a beginning-of-semester survey that they learned most effectively when visuals were included. This act of revision honored that input—albeit late—and it also provided an opportunity to take individual student struggles and input and apply them to the full class. Just as individual student understanding of power and place improved, so too did full class conversations about the different meanings of those words between cultures. As we engaged visual images as a pathway to better understanding indigenous metaphysics and epistemological forms, it became clearer to me that facilitating student engagement with diverse ideas is as important and necessary as facilitating interactions with peers. This is easy to overlook given our passion for and the value of student interactions with each other. Yet, interaction with diverse ideas is a powerful way of reinforcing recognition of the intellectual strengths of diverse non-Western cultures and disrupting historical practices of denying or overlooking such strengths.

A Final Reflection on the Why of Intercultural Teaching: Amy

Taylor was a student in the first course I ever taught, a section of College Writing. My week-long orientation to teach writing had suggested that my job was to support the development of confident and capable writers, to let students claim and find intellectual merit in their perspectives and experiences. By the end of the term, Taylor was certainly a better writer—she liked writing more; described a new, relaxed attitude toward writing; and had produced many successful essays for our class and for other classes. She felt more confident. So, we had both done our jobs. Except that, as Taylor's comment ahead makes clear, something important was missing and the work we did together didn't really "matter" in the ways I believe education should matter:

> I just don't see how we can change anything. I mean, I'm only 18 but even if I live until I'm 80, I feel like I can't really make a difference. Everything seems done already. Like racism, it just is—it's everywhere—inside. The same with the Gulf War, even if I disagree, I can't do anything about it, it's out of my reach. (Taylor, a student in my Fall, 1990 College Writing Course) (Lee, 2001, p. 27)

Taylor has stayed with me for 26 years—indeed, my first book (*Composing Critical Pedagogies*) opened with her words. She wrote her comment in response to a student-initiated discussion about the imminent Gulf War. I always collect students' impressions and reflections after course discussions or workshops as a way to notice and to report back on broad themes or points of confusion and so as to review and reflect on later in the semester with students. We can ask, "What, if anything, has changed for you?" In her final self-assessment, Taylor described herself as a more confident, authoritative writer and a more engaged learner. And yet, her notecard following this course discussion articulates a sense of impotence or detachment in things that matter to her in a broader civic, political, and social sphere. Even though she responded during the discussion to the possibility of war with affect and intellectual energy, her comment afterward describes her in a stuck position, trapped in a sense of frustration and immobility, uncertain as to how change might be effected or where to direct her energy.

She is not only describing but also ensuring her powerlessness by declaring it to be inevitable. This is not unfamiliar: students (and teachers) can easily fall into the habit of adopting powerlessness (not enough time, not enough voice, not enough resources, not enough knowledge, not enough data, not enough authority . . .). Declaring yourself detached or unable may also serve to let you off the hook from accepting accountability and responsibility for knowing or doing.

Of course, a spectrum exists among students, as among any group, in terms of their learned, perceived, and adopted senses of authority and power—in and outside of the class. Early in my teaching, I also thought a lot about another type of student I encountered, seemingly the opposite of Taylor, yet limited by the same inability to envision and reflect on connections between self and other, words and worlds. I was struck by the ease with which these writers claimed authority and knowledge. Often their essays relied on sweeping generalization, the assumption of "rational" readers who would easily assent to their articulation of universal truths, and loud, very confident, unproblematized voices. John Schilb notes in "Pedagogy of the Oppressors?" (1985) a critical pedagogy cannot be positioned as only "for" those who are institutionally "marginalized," or "disadvantaged." We must also articulate strategies for educating those of us who easily or "naturally" occupy positions of authority and privilege, strategies that challenge them to recognize how privilege is constructed and conveyed by economic and ideological conditions and through discourse, rather than based on inherent right or the "natural" order of things. Expertise is not static.

Intercultural pedagogy is about challenging ourselves and our students to interrogate the way in which we claim or resist authority and to teach one another to examine the unspoken assumptions upon which our sense of identity and interrelation, as well as self and other, is based.

Conclusion and Moving Forward

We have been clear from the onset that this book is a tool for educators who are ready to engage in the process of developing an intercultural pedagogy. The content and stories in this chapter provide an honest discussion of the critical importance of this work as well as the opportunities we have to teach our students to become critical and reflective examiners. We reiterate that this requires ongoing attention and investment, reflection and revision. None of us "arrives" and can be afforded the luxury of resting on our laurels. New situations create new contexts in and through which ideas of inclusiveness and equity can be examined and learned; new cohorts of learners bring different sets of characteristics and experiences that interact with the new contexts. As teachers, this means that we must be vigilant, responsive, flexible, and intentional about what and how we teach. Engaging with an intercultural pedagogy facilitates this ongoing process.

Throughout this book, we note the value of cultivating a community of reflective practitioners with whom to share the joys, frustrations, successes, failures, revisions, and ongoing restlessness that accompany commitment to and the practice of intercultural pedagogy. In creating this book, we became a quartet of reflective practitioners who quickly learned the value of sharing our pedagogical stories in ways that promoted our own learning, reduced the loneliness that often accompanies trying something new and confronting entrenched practice, eased the anxiety that comes with failure, and celebrated our pedagogical successes. While retaining and valuing our individual characteristics as teachers and learners and respecting our disciplinary differences, it became increasingly possible for us to challenge and question each other in productive ways regarding how and why we do what we do in classrooms and how our pedagogies honor or diminish the presence of student diversity. We actively read, shared resources, wrote, reflected, and engaged in pedagogical revision together, even though we mostly reside in different academic departments and are located on separate campuses of our university. The value of our small community of reflective practitioners causes us to encourage you to seek a community that will in a similar fashion encourage and sustain you as you remain restless in pursuing ever more effective ways to use intercultural pedagogy.

Our hope is that you will keep this book as a source of values, steps, examples, questions, and encouragement as you revise course assignments, syllabi, assessments, and other pedagogical tools. We want the book to be practical and accessible as you engage the very real work of ongoing revision in teaching and learning. Know that we too will continue in this journey of pushing ourselves to further improve in our engagement of diverse students and the honoring of their value in our own university.

REFERENCES

Andrews, T., & Burke, F. (2007). What does it mean to think historically? *Perspectives on History: The Newsmagazine of the American Historical Association, 45*(1), 32–35.

Apple, M. W. (1982). *Education and power.* New York, NY: Routledge & Kegan Paul.

Apple, M. W. (1990). *Ideology and curriculum.* New York, NY: Routledge.

Apple, M. W. (2015). Education and discomfort: On being a critical scholar/activist in education. In B. J. Porfilio & D. R. Ford (Eds.), *Leaders in critical pedagogy: Narratives for understanding and solidarity* (pp. 185–198). Boston, MA: Sense.

Ayers, E. L. (2005). *What caused the Civil War?: Reflections on the South and southern history.* New York: W.W. Norton.

Baldwin, J. (1963, December 21). A talk to teachers. *The Saturday Review* (note: originally delivered October 16, 1963, as "The Negro Child–His Self-Image"). Retrieved from http://richgibson.com/talktoteachers.htm

Barzun, J., & Graff, H. F. (1977). *The modern researcher.* New York, NY: Harcourt Brace Jovanovich.

Bennett, J. M. (2009). Cultivating intercultural competence. In D. K. Deardorff (Ed.), *The SAGE handbook of intercultural competence* (pp. 121–140). Thousand Oaks, CA: SAGE.

Bennett, M. J. (1993). Towards ethnorelativism: A developmental model of intercultural sensitivity. In R. M. Paige (Ed.), *Education for the intercultural experience* (pp. 21–71). Yarmouth, ME: Intercultural Press.

Bloch, M. (1953). *The historian's craft.* New York, NY: Vintage Books.

Bok, D. (2006). *Our underachieving colleges: A candid look at how much students learn and why they should be learning more.* Princeton, NJ: Princeton University Press.

Boler, M. (1999). *Feeling power: Emotions and education.* New York, NY: Routledge.

Brown v. Board of Education, 347 U.S. 483 (1954).

Bubolz, M. M., & Sontag, M. S. (1993). Human ecology theory. In P. G. Boss, W. J. Doherty, R. LaRossa, W. R. Schumm, & S. K. Steinmetz (Eds.), *Sourcebook of family theories and methods: A contextual approach* (pp. 419–450). New York, NY: Plenum Press.

Calder, L. (2006). Uncoverage: Toward a signature pedagogy for the history survey. *The Journal of American History, 92,* 1358–1370.

Calder, L., Cutler, W. W., & Mills Kelly, T. (2002). History lessons: Historians and the scholarship of teaching and learning. In M. T. Huber & S. P. Morreale (Eds.), *Disciplinary styles in the scholarship of teaching and learning: Exploring common ground* (pp. 45–68). Washington, DC: American Association for Higher Education & The Carnegie Foundation for the Advancement of Teaching.

Carr, E. H. (1961). *What is history?* New York, NY: Vintage Books.

Chavez, A. F. (2010). Toward a multicultural ecology of teaching and learning: A critical review of theory and research. *Journal on Excellence in College Teaching, 21*(4), 49–74.

Collins, T. (1997). For openers . . . An inclusive course syllabus. In W. E. Campbell & K. A. Smith (Eds.), *New paradigms for college teaching* (pp. 79–102). Edina, MN: Interaction Book.

Commager, H. S. (1965). *The nature and the study of history.* Columbus, OH: Charles E. Merrill Books.

Cook-Sather, A. (2015). Dialogue Across Differences of Position, Perspective, and Identity. *Teachers College Record, 117*(February), 1–42.

Cranton, P. (2001). *Becoming an authentic teacher in higher education.* Malabar, FL: Krieger.

Cranton, P. (2006). *Understanding and promoting transformative learning: A guide for educators of adults* (2nd ed.). San Francisco, CA: John Wiley & Sons.

Deardorff, D. K. (2006). Identification and assessment of intercultural competence as a student outcome of internationalization. *Journal of Studies in International Education, 10*(3), 241.

Deloria, V., Jr., & Wildcat, D. R. (2001). *Power and place: Indian education in America.* Golden, CO: Fulcrum Resources.

Dey, E. L., Ott, M. C., Antonaros, M., Barnhardt, C. L., & Holsapple, M. A. (2010). *Engaging diverse viewpoints: What is the campus climate for perspective-taking?* Washington, DC: American Association of Colleges and Universities.

Dirkx, J. M. (1998). Transformative learning theory in the practice of adult education: An overview. *PAACE Journal of Lifelong Learning, 7,* 1–14.

Du Bois, W. E. B. (1903/1994). *The souls of Black folk.* Mineola, NY: Dover Thrift Editions.

Eisenchlas, S. A., & Trevaskes, S. (2003). Teaching intercultural communication in the university setting: An Australian perspective. *Intercultural Education, 14*(4), 397–408.

Ellison, R. (1952). *Invisible man.* New York, NY: Random House.

Elton, G. R. (1967). *The practice of history.* New York, NY: Thomas Y. Cromwell.

Evans, R. J. (1999). *In defense of history.* New York, NY: W.W. Norton.

Fantini, A. (2009). Assessing intercultural competence: Issues and tools. In D. K. Deardorff (Ed.), *The SAGE handbook of intercultural competence* (pp. 456–476). Thousand Oaks, CA: SAGE.

Fink, L. D. (2003). *Creating significant learning experiences: An integrated approach to designing college courses.* San Francisco, CA: Jossey-Bass.

Fink, L. D. (2013). *Creating significant learning experiences: An integrated approach to designing college courses—revised and updated.* San Francisco, CA: Jossey-Bass.

Fischer, D. H. (1970). *Historians' fallacies: Toward a logic of historical thought.* New York, NY: Harper Perennial.

Franklin, J. H. (2005). *Mirror to America: The autobiography of John Hope Franklin.* New York, NY: Farrar, Straus & Giroux.

Franklin, J. H., & J. W. Franklin (Eds.). (1997). *My life and an era: The autobiography of Buck Colbert Franklin.* Baton Rouge, LA: Louisiana State University Press.

Franklin, J. H. (2005). *Mirror to America: The autobiography of John Hope Franklin.* New York, NY: Farrar, Straus and Giroux.

Freire, P. (1970). *Pedagogy of the oppressed.* New York, NY: Penguin Books.

Freire, P. (1973). *Education for critical consciousness.* New York, NY: Seabury.

Freire, P. (1998). *Teachers as cultural workers: Letters to those who dare teach.* Boulder, CO: Westview Press.

Gesche, A., & Makeham, P. (2008). Creating conditions for intercultural and international learning and teaching. In M. Hellstén & A. M. Reid (Eds.), *Researching international pedagogies: Sustainable practice for teaching and learning in higher education* (pp. 241–258). New York: Springer.

Gore, J. (1992). What we can do for you! What can "we" do for "you"? Struggling over empowerment in critical and feminist pedagogy. In C. Luke & J. Gore (Eds.), *Feminisms and critical pedagogy* (pp. 54–73). New York, NY: Routledge.

Gurung, R. A. R., Chick, N., & Haynie, A. (2009). From generic to signature pedagogies. In R. A. R. Gurung, N. Chick, & A. Haynie (Eds.), *Exploring signature pedagogies: Approaches to teaching disciplinary habits of mind* (pp. 1–18). Sterling, VA: Stylus.

Handlin, O. (1979). *Truth in history.* Cambridge, MA: The Belknap Press of Harvard University Press.

Harari, M. (1992). Internationalization of the curriculum. In C. B. Klasek (Ed.), *Bridges to the future: Strategies for internationalizing higher education* (pp. 52–79). Carbondale, IL: Association of International Education Administrators.

Hook, J. N., Davis, D. E., Owen, J., Worthington, E. L. & Utsey, S. O. (2013). Cultural humility: Measuring openness to culturally diverse clients. *Journal of Counseling Psychology, 6*(3), 353–366.

hooks, b. (1994). *Teaching to transgress: Education as the practice of freedom.* New York, NY: Routledge.

Horner, B., & Lu, M. Z. (1999). *Representing the "other": Basic writers and the teaching of basic writing.* Urbana, IL: National Council of Teachers of English.

Katila, S., Merilainen, S., & Tienarirefer, J. (2010). *Making inclusion work: Experiences from academia and around the world.* Cheltenham, UK: Edward Elgar.

Kim, Y. Y. (2005). Association and dissociation: A contextual theory of interethnic communication. In W. B. Gudykunst (Ed.), *Theorizing about intercultural communication* (pp. 323–349). London: SAGE.

Kim, Y. Y. (2009). The identity factor in intercultural competence. In D. K. Deardorff (Ed.), *The SAGE handbook of intercultural competence* (pp. 53–65). London: SAGE.

Krutky, J. (2008). Intercultural competency: Preparing students to be global citizens. *Effective Practices for Academic Leaders, 3*(1), 1–15.

Langer, E. (1997). *The power of mindful learning.* New York, NY: Addison-Wesley.

Lattery, M. J. (2009). Signature pedagogies in introductory physics. In R. A. R. Guring, N. L. Chick, & A. Haynie (Eds.), *Exploring signature pedagogies: Approaches to teaching disciplinary habits of mind* (pp. 280–294). Sterling, VA: Stylus.

Leask, B. (2009). Using formal and informal curricula to improve interactions between home and international students. *Journal of Studies in International Education, 13*(2), 205–211.

Lee, A. (2001). *Composing critical pedagogies: Teaching writing as revision.* Urbana, IL: NCTE.

Lee, A., Poch, R., Williams, R. D., & Shaw, M. (2012). *Engaging diversity in undergraduate classrooms: A pedagogy for developing intercultural competence.* Association for the Study of Higher Education Series. San Francisco, CA: Jossey-Bass.

Lee, A., & Williams, R. D. (Eds.). (2017). *Engaging dissonance: Pedagogy for mindful global citizenship in higher education.* London, UK: Emerald Group.

Lee, A., Williams, R. D., Shaw, M., & Jie, Y. (2014). First year students' perspectives on intercultural learning. *Teaching in Higher Education, 19*(5), 543–554.

Lerner, G. (1997). *Why history matters: Life and thought.* New York, NY: Oxford University Press.

Liebowitz, R. D. (2007, May 26). The value of discomfort: Baccalaureate address to the class of 2007. Middlebury, VT: Middlebury College. Retrieved from http://www.middlebury.edu/about/president/addresses_archive_copy/archive/baccalaureate2007/node/470112

Loewen, J. W. (1995). *Lies my teacher told me: Everything your American history textbook got wrong.* New York, NY: Touchstone.

Lusted, D. (1986). Why pedagogy? *Screen, 27*(5), 2–16.

Marius, R., & Page, M. E. (2005). *A short guide to writing about history.* New York, NY: Pearson Longman.

Marx, K., Engels, F., Moore, S., & McLellan, D. (1848). *The Communist manifesto.*

McDermott, R., & Varenne, H. (1995). Culture as disability. *Anthropology and Education Quarterly, 26*(3), 324–348.

Merriam, S. B., & Associates (2007). *Non-Western perspectives on learning and knowing.* Malabar, FL: Krieger.

Mestenhauser, J. A. (2011). *Reflections on the past, present, and future of internationalizing higher education: Discovering opportunities to meet challenges.* Minneapolis, MN: Global Programs & Strategy Alliance, University of Minnesota.

Mezirow, J. (1990). *Fostering critical reflection in adulthood: A guide to transformative and emancipatory learning.* San Francisco, CA: Jossey Bass.

Mezirow, J. (1997). Transformative learning: Theory to practice. *New Directions for Adult and Continuing Education, 74*, 5–12.

Milem, J. F., Chang, M. J., & Antonio, A. L. (2005). *Making diversity work on campus: A research-based perspective.* Washington, DC: Association of American Colleges and Universities.

Nevins, A. (1963). *The gateway to history.* Chicago, IL: Quadrangle Books.

North, S. M. (1987). *The making of knowledge in composition: Portrait of an emerging field.* Upper Montclair, NJ: Boynton/Cook.

Rampolla, M. L. (2015). *A pocket guide to writing in history.* New York, NY: Bedford/St. Martin's.

Rendón, L. I. (1992). From the barrio to the academy: Revelations of a Mexican American scholarship girl. *New Directions for Community Colleges, 80*, 55–64.

Rendón, L. I. (2009). *Sentipensante (sensing/thinking) pedagogy: Educating for wholeness, social justice and liberation.* Sterling, VA: Stylus.

Rich, A. (1986). *Blood, bread, and poetry: Selected prose 1979–1985.* New York, NY: W. W. Norton & Company.

Russo, T. C., & Ford, D. J. (2006). Teachers' reflection on reflection practice. *Journal of Cognitive Affective Learning, 2*(2), 1–12.

Sanderson, G. (2008). A foundation for the internationalisation of the academic self. *Journal of Studies in International Education, 12*(3), 276–307.

Sanderson, G. (2009, June). *The secret lives of internationalized lecturers: A detective's story.* Paper presented at Internationalising the Home Student CICIN conference. Oxford Brookes University, UK.

Schilb, J. "Pedagogy of the oppressors?" (1985). In M. Culley & C. Portuges (Eds.), *Gendered subjects: The dynamics of feminist teaching* (pp. 253–264). Boston, MA: Routledge.

Selasi, T. (2015, October 25). *Don't ask me where I'm from, ask where I'm a local* [Video file]. Retrieved from https://youtu.be/LYCKzpXEW6E

Shor, I. (1999). What is critical literacy? In A. Darder, M. Baltodano, & R. D. Torres (Eds.), *The critical pedagogy reader* (pp. 282–304). London: RoutledgeFalmer.

Simon, R. (1988). Empowerment as a pedagogy of possibility. *Language Arts, 64*(4), 370–382.

Sipress, J. M., & Voelker, D. J. (2009). From learning history to doing history. In R. A. R. Guring, N. L. Chick, & A. Haynie (Eds.), *Exploring signature pedagogies: Approaches to teaching disciplinary habits of mind* (pp. 19–35). Sterling, VA: Stylus.

Smith, D. G. (2010). *Diversity's promise for higher education.* Baltimore, MD: The Johns Hopkins University Press.

Stenberg, S., & Lee, A. (2002). Developing pedagogies: Learning the teaching of English. *College English, 64*(3), 326–347.

Stern, F. (Ed.). (1973). *The varieties of history: From Voltaire to the present.* New York, NY: Vintage Books.

Takaki, R. (1993). *A different mirror: A history of multicultural America.* Boston, MA: Little, Brown.

Ting-Toomey, S. (2005). Identity negotiation theory: Crossing cultural boundaries. In W. B. Gudykunst (Ed.), *Theorizing about intercultural communication* (pp. 211–233). Thousand Oaks, CA: SAGE.

Tuchman, B. (1981). *Practicing history.* New York, NY: Alfred A. Knopf.

Wells, H. G. (1904/1911). *The country of the blind and other stories.* London, UK: Thomas Nelson and Sons.

Wood, G. (2008). *The purpose of the past: Reflections on the uses of history.* New York, NY: The Penguin Press.

CONTRIBUTORS

Amy Lee is a professor at the University of Minnesota. Her PhD is in English/composition studies. Her scholarship focuses on teacher-education for postsecondary faculty with a goal of supporting equity, diversity, and inclusive excellence in college classrooms. She has published six books in this area and a number of articles. Lee has taught a range of graduate and undergraduate courses, including first year writing and basic writing; U.S. literature; multicultural education; doctoral seminars in composition theory and research methods, and critical pedagogy. She has served in program- and department-level leadership positions at multiple public universities, and received university teaching awards from the University of Massachusetts–Amherst and the University of Minnesota.

Robert Poch is a senior fellow in the Department of Curriculum and Instruction at the University of Minnesota. He teaches undergraduate history and graduate courses in postsecondary multicultural teaching and learning and college student development theory. His current research focuses on problem-based approaches to teaching history within diverse classrooms. Patch is a recipient of the Horace T. Morse University of Minnesota Alumni Association Award for Outstanding Contributions to Undergraduate Education. He holds a PhD in higher education from the University of Virginia.

Mary Katherine O'Brien is a researcher for education and outreach in the College of Veterinary Medicine at the University of Minnesota. She has worked in the field of international education since 2002, holding positions in the areas of international student advising, education abroad, internationalization of the on-campus curriculum, and international program development. O'Brien holds a PhD in comparative and international development education and focused on the academic engagement and classroom learning experiences of undergraduate international students for her dissertation. She conducts research on the internationalization of higher education, cross-border partnerships, online education, and the intercultural aspects of teaching and learning.

Catherine Solheim is a faculty member in the Department of Family Social Science at the University of Minnesota. She teaches graduate and undergraduate courses on family finances, family theory, and global and diverse families. She has led multiple learning abroad courses to Thailand, focusing on how globalization impacts family, communities, culture, and the natural environment. Solheim studies ways that culture, socioeconomic status, and relationships impact the diverse ways families make decisions about their resources. She has conducted research on decision-making in Thai families, transnational Mexican-Minnesotan, family resource and relationship decisions, and the values and financial practices of two-generation Hmong immigrant families in Minnesota. Her current research examines mental health and economic transitions of newly arrived refugee families from Burma (Myanmar) using a collaborative community-based research approach. This research has a keen aim to contribute to systems and policy changes that improve refugee family transitions and well-being.

problem creating by, 66–69
reflection with, 37, 71–73, 84–85,
    87, 88–91, 94–95, 103, 120–21
satisfaction of, 5, 59, 68, 74
survey of, 70
as teachers, 49
voices of, 57, 63–64, 71, 72–75,
    95–96, 120

Takaki, Ronald, 49, 61
"A Talk to Teachers" (Baldwin), 99
teachers
    authentic, 24
    environment as, 118
    self as, 39–41
    students as, 49
teaching
    assessment of, 19, 22
    assistantships in, 8
    content focus of, 22, 40, 41, 42, 46,
        49–50, 53, 79–81
    context for, 87
    disciplinary focus in, 18–19
    disenfranchisement of, 19
    efficiency of, 4
    experimentation in, 81
    as facilitating, 59
    humility in, 95
    intentionality in, 13–14, 21, 22–23,
        122
    modeling in, 100
    multidisciplinary approach to, 16,
        99–100
    pedagogy as different from, 14
    responsibility of, 99–100
    signature pedagogies for, 51
    as supplement, 6, 7
    tensions in, 49–50, 77–78
    tools for curriculum development,
        77, 100
    training for, 7–8, 18–19, 42, 87
    transformation of, 46
    visuals in, 88, 119–20

technology
    investments in, 7
    as research tool, 53, 58
TED talk, 94
tenure, 39
textbooks, 60, 61–62
Thailand, 32–33, 37–38, 95, 97
"3Rs: Relationships, Rituals, and
    Restrictions" (Selasi), 94
transformationalist, 112

United States Agency for International
    Development (USAID), 32
United States (U.S)
    diversity in, 4, 21
    reflection on, 36
unlearning, 25
U.S. See United States
USAID. See United States Agency for
    International Development
Utsey, S. O., 24

Varenne, Herve, vii
Vietnam War, 70–71
Virginia, 51
visuals, 88, 119–20
voices
    in history, 75–76
    of students, 57, 63–64, 71, 72–75,
        95–96, 120
volunteering, 84, 105–6

Washington, DC, 34
Washington Avenue Bridge, 109
Wells, H. G., vii
"What the Black Man Wants"
    (Douglass), 52–53
Wildcat, Daniel, 16, 20, 118
words, context of, 117, 118–19
Worthington, E. L., 24
writing, 73

Zitkala-Sa, 62

inclusive classrooms that honor each learner's identity and support education for social justice. Her book is vital reading for anyone seeking to create more inclusive institutions for students and teachers alike."—*Diversity & Democracy (AAC&U)*

"Challenging, inspiring, beautifully written, and unusual, this book calls readers to find ways to link mind and heart—thinking and feeling—to transform teaching and learning in higher education. . . . The book or any of its individual chapters can be used by individuals thinking through their own values and practice, in classes designed to prepare future faculty members, or in faculty development programs organizing dialogues about teaching and academic life. . . . [This book is] an important, thought-provoking, and unique addition to the literature on teaching, learning, and the academic life."—*The Review of Higher Education*

Sty/us

22883 Quicksilver Drive
Sterling, VA 20166-2102   Subscribe to our e-mail alerts: www.Styluspub.com

Also available from Stylus

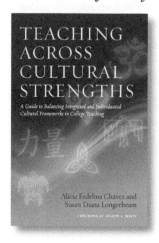

Teaching Across Cultural Strengths
A Guide to Balancing Integrated and Individuated Cultural Frameworks in College Teaching
Alicia Fedelina Chávez and Susan Diana Longerbeam

Foreword by Joseph L. White

"Why aren't student success rates in college even across cultural groups? Chávez and Longerbeam unpack this mystery with an insightful and very usable set of ideas for faculty who want to teach to student strengths and support success across cultures. They provide a comprehensive framework for understanding culture and pedagogy. This is an outstanding book that should be read by all faculty members who are puzzled by differences in their ability to relate to students from different backgrounds and by differential rates of success. A huge contribution."
—Jane Fried, Professor, Central Connecticut State University

"This book offers a comprehensive set of guidelines based on a sound theoretical foundation and empirical research that will enable college teachers to narrow the gap in cross cultural teaching and student learning and assist teachers in transforming learning for all students across the many cultures that exist in the classroom. By following the steps outlined in this book, teachers can progressively learn about the role of culture in learning while transforming their teaching through introspection, reflection, practice, and the application of new teaching pedagogies that deepen student learning."*—Joseph L. White, Professor Emeritus of Psychology and Psychiatry, University of California, Irvine*

Sentipensante (Sensing/Thinking) Pedagogy
Educating for Wholeness, Social Justice and Liberation
Laura I. Rendón

Foreword by Mark Nepo

"What would happen if educators eschewed the silent agreements that govern institutions and established a new set of working assumptions that honor the fullness of humanity? In this visionary study, Laura Rendón lays the groundwork for a pedagogy that bridges the gap between mind and heart to lead students and educators toward a new conception of teaching and learning. Grounding her work in interviews of scholars who are already transforming the educational landscape, Rendón invites the reader to join a burgeoning movement toward more

(Continued on preceding page)